Up, Down, Move Around
Nutrition and Motor Skills

Active Learning for Preschoolers

by Deborah Kayton Michals

Dedication

This book is dedicated to the inspirational examples and memories of my mother, Marjorie Kayton—a creative and passionately committed preschool music and movement teacher; and my grandmother, Lillian Klempner—a dedicated teacher who practiced fitness and nutritional awareness to age 102.

Acknowledgements

I express my grateful appreciation in particular to Megan Bascom for her essential work in the research, organization, and writing of these books; to Angessa Hughmanick, Kimberly Lantz, and Carmen Marrett for their contributions; to Phyllis Lyons for her support and viewpoint; and to Marian Tanofsky-Kraff, Meghan O'Connell, and Christina Roberto for their assistance with the nutritional material. Thanks very much to my editor, Stephanie Roselli, and to Clarissa Willis and the Gryphon House team for their work, and to Kathy Charner and Melinda Scrivner for their encouragement. Thanks to Alan Lopatin, lobbyist on behalf of young children and others who can't advocate for themselves, whose work brought these books into existence. And thanks to my husband, Jonathan Michals, and children, Ali, Ben, and Katie, who inspire me daily.

Up, Down, Move Around

Nutrition and Motor Skills

Active Learning for Preschoolers

Deborah Kayton Michals

Gryphon House
Lewisville, NC

Copyright

Published by Gryphon House, Inc.
P. O. Box 10, Lewisville, NC 27023
800.638.0928; 877.638.7576 (fax)

Visit us on the web at www.gryphonhouse.com.

Library of Congress Cataloging-in-Publication Data

Michals, Deborah Kayton.
 Up, down, move around : nutrition and motor skills : active learning for preschoolers / by Deborah Kayton Michals.
    pages cm
 Includes bibliographical references and index.
 ISBN 978-0-87659-471-1
 1. Health education--Activity programs. 2. School children--Nutrition. 3. Early childhood education. I. Title.
 LB1140.5.H4M53 2013
 613.071--dc23
                              2012042085

Bulk Purchase

Gryphon House books are available for special premiums and sales promotions as well as for fund-raising use. Special editions or book excerpts also can be created to specifications. For details, contact the Director of Marketing at Gryphon House.

Disclaimer

Table of Contents

Introduction

Well-balanced nutrition and physical activity are key components of a healthy lifestyle. *Up, Down, Move Around–Nutrition and Motor Skills: Active Learning for Preschoolers* offers practical, easy-to-use ideas that fit seamlessly into your already-packed classroom schedule.

The nutrition activities are designed to help you address nutritional requirements and standards:
- Teach children what a healthy, well-balanced diet is.
- Provide lots of opportunities for children to learn about and explore healthy foods.
- Offer children developmentally appropriate food-related activities.
- Broaden children's food experiences.

You can easily adapt the activities in this book to emphasize the healthy, available, and locally grown foods that make up a well-balanced diet in your area. The exercises uniquely combine nutritional learning with physical activity so that children are accomplishing goals in both areas.

Many physical fitness and nutrition programs separate the two components. The nexus of physical activity and contextual learning in the exercises can be an optimal, engaging, and enjoyable way of teaching preschoolers about healthy nutrition and exercise. By linking nutrition to physical fitness and motor skills, the preschooler will understand the idea that healthy eating and physical fitness go together.

Up, Down, Move Around–Nutrition and Motor Skills: Active Learning for Preschoolers provides the tools to help you develop gross and fine motor skills through fun, noncompetitive activities.

- Encourage children to explore their physical strengths and abilities.
- Create an atmosphere in which all ability levels are respected and accepted.
- Reach children who do not respond well to more sedentary activities or listening while sitting.
- If there are children in your class who have special needs, use the activities to highlight positive aspects of the way they learn.
- Reach English-language learners by helping them associate concepts with words before they actually know the vocabulary.

Preschool children need to move, and physical activity is a proven pathway to cognitive learning for this age group. Active play provides the most effective learning for preschoolers, giving you wonderful opportunities to influence children's learning in both hemispheres of the brain. Active learning sharpens auditory discrimination and multiple-intelligence learning as children listen to and process information, translating that information into physical activity. A child's attention becomes more focused during physical activity, and a great learning opportunity exists at this peak of focus.

I started out as a young teacher and dancer, teaching movement education in motor-skill development, creative thinking, self-confidence, and problem solving. As I taught, directed programs, and trained others over the course of more than 25 years, I saw that it was possible to use these methods to teach essential material from the rest of the preschool day. My experience integrating these aspects of action and learning inspired me to incorporate fitness, body awareness, and obesity prevention into a total-child approach. Then, First Lady Michelle Obama's 2009 "Let's Move" public-awareness campaign motivated development of this book, a user-friendly guide to incorporate children's movements in developing their cognitive abilities.

According to a report issued by the Robert Wood Johnson Foundation, more than 21 percent of preschool children in the United States are overweight or obese, and poor diet and lack of physical exercise are contributing factors. To combat childhood obesity, teaching children physical fitness from an early age is essential. If you teach children about nutrition and motor-skill exercises, you increase children's lifelong awareness of the importance of proper nutrition and physical fitness. By incorporating physical activity seamlessly into the structure of the school day, it naturally becomes an integral part of how children learn, how they grow, and how they think and feel about their bodies. The body is a child's first playground, and by connecting it clearly to the learning process, it can remain so in a world in which technology competes for their attention.

How to Use the Exercises

These exercises are keyed to specific research components—exposure to foods, social influence of peer and adult role models, and eating patterns—that have shown results in encouraging preschool children to learn about nutrition and make healthy food choices.

The exercises combine learning in nutrition with physical action so that children connect nutritional awareness with the physical fitness of their bodies. The motor-skill exercises utilize innovative creative structures and games for a noncompetitive fitness curriculum that can be done in any classroom.

The exercises are flexible and easy to incorporate into your classroom routine:

- No special materials, props, or extra space are required. Everything you need is already in your classroom!
- Exercises can be done as 5- to 10-minute enrichment activities with your regular curriculum lesson.
- Activities can be extended from 10 to 20 minutes to use as self-contained lessons.
- Exercises can be stacked, in groups of two to five, for up to an hour's worth of physical activity.
- Use the exercises toward the 60 minutes of structured physical activity recommended for preschoolers in national guidelines, and complement your standard physical fitness games and exercises.*
- Use the activities with large and small groups, in circle time, and as transitions. Small-group time allows for more particularized attention to the individual child; whereas, whole-group exercises benefit from the high energy level and multiple shapes and suggestions of a larger group.

Up, Down, Move Around–Nutrition and Motor Skills: Active Learning for Preschoolers presents solutions to the problem of fitting enough physical activity into your school day. Give the children in your classroom the physical activity and fitness they need while learning and working toward meeting your goals in nutrition and motor skills. Enjoy moving the children and yourself with productive action throughout the day!

*National Association for Sports and Physical Education. 2009. *Active Start: A Statement of Physical Activity Guidelines for Children from Birth to Age 5,* 2nd ed. Reston, VA: NASPE.

Move for Nutritional Learning

This Is the Way We Eat Our Meal

Teach the children the progression of mealtime and a slow, healthy rhythm of eating.

How to Do It

1. Teach the children the following song, sung to the tune of "Here We Go 'Round the Mulberry Bush."

   We get ready to eat our meal

   Eat our meal, eat our meal.

   We get ready to eat our meal

   So we can have our snacktime. (or breakfast, lunchtime, dinner)

   This is the way we wash our hands

   Wash our hands, wash our hands.

   This is the way we wash our hands

   So we can have our snacktime.

   This is the way we set out the plates

   Set out the plates, set out the plates.

   This is the way we set out the plates

   So we can have our snacktime.

2. Continue singing, adding stanzas to describe the steps of eating: set out our cups, place our forks, sit at the table, use our forks, chew our food, drink our water, clear our plates, wash our plates, and so forth.

3. Sing the song again, miming the actions.

Expand It!

Encourage the children to sing this song when they play in the home living center or as the class prepares for mealtime.

Eat Breakfast! Eat Breakfast!

Use this fun call-and-response to reinforce the importance of eating a healthy breakfast in the morning.

How to Do It

1. While standing, start by tapping a steady beat on your legs.
2. Teach the children the following call-and-response:

   Teacher: What do you do when you get up?

   Children: Eat breakfast! Eat breakfast! (shimmy and shake head and body side to side)

   Teacher: What do you do when you start the day?

   Children: Eat breakfast! Eat breakfast! (shimmy and shake)

   Teacher: What do you do after you get dressed?

   Children: Eat breakfast! Eat breakfast! (shimmy and shake)

   Teacher: What do you do to have a good day?

   Children: Eat breakfast! Eat breakfast! (shimmy and shake)

   All Together: Eating breakfast every day is the way I feel okay!

   Eating breakfast every day is the way I say hurray! (Jump up in air)

Expand It!

Talk about the foods that make a good breakfast: oatmeal and milk with fruit, yogurt and cereal, eggs and toast, and pancakes. Ask the children to share their ideas about what makes a healthy breakfast.

Wash Your Hands Dance

Teach children healthy hygiene habits and develop their cross-patterning mobility.

How to Do It

1. Invite the children stand in a circle with feet hip-distance apart in a comfortable position.
2. Ask them to act out the following directions:

   Pick up the soap (pretend to pick up a bar of soap)

   And turn on the water. (pretend to turn on faucet)

   Wash your hands (Rub hands for eight counts)

   And shake them off. (Shake hands with open fingers for eight counts)

   Wash them high, (Rub hands together overhead)

   Wash them low, (Rub hands together as you lean over)

   Shake them to the left, (Turn to left and shake hands as if flinging water)

   Shake them to the right. (Turn to right and shake hands as if flinging water)

   Shake them, shake them (Shake hands with open fingers for eight counts)

   With all of your might! Grab a towel, (Mimic reaching for a towel)

   Dry them well, (Clap hands right, then left)

   Clean and neat (Extend right arm, then left. Cross arms touching hands to opposite shoulders)

   Let's eat! (Open arms, close arms, and clap hands)

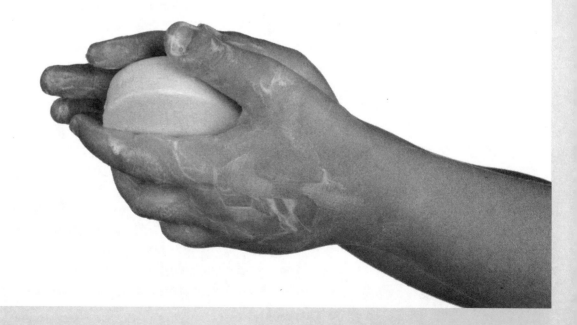

I Help Set Up and Clean Up

Reinforce responsibility, self-respect, fine motor skills, and math skills of one-to-one correspondence and patterns—all by setting the table!

How to Do It

1. This activity works well with small groups of children, and it is a great way to use placemats that the children make themselves.
2. On a table, provide enough placemats, plates, cups, forks, spoons, and napkins for all of the children in the group.
3. Set one place setting on the table where the children eat their meals. Include a placemat, plate, cup, fork, spoon, and napkin. Ask the children to notice the elements of the place setting.
4. Say, "It's time to set the table! What do we need?" Listen as the children offer their suggestions:
   - Placemats! Where do they go? In front of each chair.
   - What comes next? Plates! Where do the plates go? One plate in the middle of each placemat.
   - Next we need napkins. Where do they go? Next to the plate on this side (point to left side).
   - Now what do we need? Forks and spoons! How many forks and spoons do we need? How many children are here in our group? We need one fork and one spoon for every child.
   - Where do the forks and spoons go? The fork goes on one side of the plate, over here (point to left side), and the spoon goes on the other side of the plate (point to right side).
   - Now what is missing? A water or milk cup. Where does it go? Above the spoon, on this side of the plate (point to the right side).
5. Say, "Look, our table is all set!" Pretend to eat, or eat a snack together.

Expand It!

Encourage the children to set the table in the home living center, or let them take turns setting the table for lunch or snack.

Yes, Please, and No, Thanks!

Reinforce social skills as you teach children to say, "Yes, please!" to healthy foods and "No, thanks!" to unhealthy foods.

How to Do It

1. Ask the children to stand in a line. Teach them how to respond when someone offers them something: to nod their heads as they say, "Yes, please!" or to shake their heads as they say, "No, thanks!"
2. Tell them they will get to practice responding politely when someone offers them food. For example, you might offer the children a healthy food, such as apple slices. Ask them how they would respond politely if they were offered apple slices: "Yes, please!" with a vigorous nod.
3. Have fun making up your own variations. Next, offer them an unhealthy food, such as fried pickles. Ask them how they would respond politely to the offer of fried pickles: "No, thanks!" with a vigorous shake of the head.

Expand It!

Ask for volunteers to offer the class a food. How will the class respond politely to each offer?

The USDA provides great information on portion sizes and well-balanced nutrition at www.ChooseMyPlate.gov.

I Serve Myself Some Food

This is a fun activity to do along with teaching about proper portion sizes and how much to eat at each meal or snack.

How to Do It

1. Ask the children to sit in a big circle.
2. Teach them the following song to the tune of "The Farmer in the Dell."
   I serve myself some food. (Use big gestures to mime serving yourself some food.)
   I serve myself some food, (Mime serving yourself some food.)
   I serve myself and that's enough,
   That's enough to eat! (Nod head)
3. Talk with them about the types of foods to eat in a well-balanced diet: fruits, vegetables, grains, proteins, and dairy. Ask them to name some of the foods from each category that they would like to eat.
4. As you discuss each food category, sing the song and pretend to serve yourselves some of those foods. For example, ask, "What proteins do you like? Chicken? fish? beans?" (Listen to the children's responses.) Say, "Yum! Let's eat!" and sing the song together:
   I serve myself some beans.
   I serve myself some beans,
   I serve myself and that's enough,
   That's enough to eat!

Expand It!

Go around the room and ask each child what his favorite food is. Have him show the actions of one verse for his classmates.

Chew-Chew!

Teach the children a calm, slow pace for eating meals.

How to Do It

1. Ask the children to sit in circle. Establish a rhythm by tapping your knees.
2. Begin with a fast rhythm. Say, "If you eat fast, your tummy will ache." Mime chewing quickly and making funny faces. Then, rub your tummy and pretend to ache.
3. Slow the rhythm and say, "But if you eat slowly, you'll feel great!" Mime slow chewing, then pat your tummy and raise your hands in a cheer, "Hooray!"
3. Repeat, asking for volunteers to lead the actions.

Expand It!

Do this activity as a transition to lunch or snacktime, or any time the children have to wait for a few minutes between activities.

The Food Rainbow

Teach the children that healthy, delicious foods come in lots of colors. The more colors we eat, the better!

How to Do It

1. Gather the children on one side of the room, and ask them if they have ever seen a rainbow. Ask them if they know some of the colors in a rainbow. Let them offer their ideas. Name any of the colors that the children do not name.
2. Say, "Let's make a rainbow." Start on one side of the room, crouched low, and raise arms up overhead as you make the arc of the rainbow as you move together across the room. Crouch again on the other side of the room.
3. Repeat the action, naming a different color (red, orange, yellow, green, blue, purple) each time.
4. Tell them that healthy foods from nature come in all the colors of the rainbow. Say, "The rainbow comes after the rain, which helps our foods of many colors grow! Let's see what colors of the rainbow come out of the ground."
4. Ask, "What foods can you think of that are red?" Encourage the children to name some foods. (Note: If a child names an artificially colored food, explain that that food does not come from nature and is not as healthy for us. Give that child another chance to name a food.)
5. As the children name foods, such as apples or tomatoes, say, "Let's find them! An apple is red. Let's go find an apple tree and pick some apples." Pretend to search around the room for an apple tree and reach up high to pick some apples.
6. Continue naming foods that are different colors of the rainbow, pretending to search for and gather them:
    - Red—apple, tomato, strawberry, raspberries, pepper
    - Orange—pumpkin, peach, cantaloupe, carrots, oranges
    - Yellow—banana, corn, pepper, lemon, pineapple
    - Green—grapes, pear, kiwi, broccoli, peas
    - Blue—blueberries
    - Purple—plum, figs, eggplant, cabbage, grapes

Expand It!

- Take the foods back to the home living center or restaurant dramatic play area and prepare them to eat, then have a "feast."
- Bring in actual foods of different colors to spark the exercise and to taste afterward.

What's on My Food Plate?

This fun song will reinforce the importance of eating healthy foods every day.

How to Do It

1. Teach the children the following song, sung to the tune of the Christmas carol "Up on the Housetop":

   What's on my food plate? (Children look at "plate" in their arms)

   Oh, let's see! (Dance around with "plate")

   Fruits and vegetables,

   Grain, and protein!

   Vegetables, fruits!

   Protein and grain!

   I'll eat it today and tomorrow again!

   (chorus)

   Oh, oh, oh! That's what I know! (nod head yes)

   Oh, oh, oh, and I can show you! (Hold "plate" out to show it)

   I'm going to eat some every day,

   Because I know I'll grow that way!

   What's on my food plate? (Children look at "plate" in their arms)

   Oh, let's see! (Dance around with "plate")

   Fruits and vegetables,

   Grain, and protein!

2. Change the categories of food to name specific foods, for example:

   What's on my food plate? (Children look at "plate" in their arms)

   Oh, let's see! (Dance around with "plate")

   Apples and carrots,

   Rice and fish!

   Broccoli, pears!

   Nuts and pasta!

Expand It!

Sing this song as a transition to meals or snacktime.

Healthy-Eating Obstacle Course

Teach children about good nutrition while reinforcing counting, pattern sequencing, and fine and gross motor skills.

How to Do It

1. Set up an obstacle course using mats, climbing wedges, and tunnels.
2. Set up five stations along the way: breakfast, morning snack, lunch, afternoon snack, and dinner. Post photos or the children's drawings of the healthy foods that can be "eaten" at each station, for example:
   - Breakfast: Children cup their hands to make a "bowl," pour cereal into bowl, pour milk into bowl, hold spoon, and eat.
   - Morning Snack: Children pretend to peel a banana and eat.
   - Lunch: Children pretend to make a sandwich using one hand as "bread," put on healthy sandwich ingredients, top with the other slice of bread (hand), and eat.
   - Afternoon Snack: Children pretend to dip carrots into hummus. Pick up carrots, dip, eat, and repeat!
   - Dinner: Children pretend to fill a healthy plate containing a protein, a grain, a vegetable, and a fruit.
3. Ask the children to begin at "home base." Practice the actions and the counting with children as a group while they stand in line for their turns. The first child will move to the first station where he will prepare a healthy breakfast. As he works, the child and the children who are waiting count the steps: One, make a bowl; two, pour cereal in the bowl; three, pour in some milk; four, hold a spoon and eat.
4. The child next moves to the morning snack station. There, the child counts the steps one through four as he peels, peels, peels, and eats a banana.
5. Child continues through each station, counting the four steps in each.
6. When he completes the dinner station, he runs to home base to wait for the rest of the children to finish the course.

Expand It!

Encourage the children to roll, jump, turn and jump, or gallop as they move through the obstacle course.

How Does the Garden Grow?

Support the children's understanding of how different plants grow.

How to Do It

1. Invite the children to join you in a circle. Teach them the following rhyme.

   Does it grow in the ground? (crouch down)

   Does it grow on a tree? (stand up and reach out with arms)

   Does it grow on a stalk? (arms reach up high)

   Oh! Let me see!

   Does it grow on a bush? (crouch down with round arms)

   Does it grow on a vine? (stand, reach out with wavy arms)

   Does it grow up a wall? (bring hands down,
        then "grow" up with arms high)

   How does it get really tall?

   When I eat all these things (sway to rhythm
        of rhyme, head side to side)

   So healthy and good

   I also will grow

   And grow like I should!

2. Name a fruit or vegetable, such as a grape. Ask the children, "How do you think it grows?" Listen to their responses, giving each child a turn to guess.

3. Tell the children how the fruit or vegetable grows: in or on the ground, a tree, a stalk, a bush, or a vine. "A grape grows on a vine!"

Water Everywhere

Support children's understanding of the water cycle and the importance of drinking enough water.

How to Do It

1. Invite the children to stand with you in a circle. Tell them, "Water is everywhere around us!" Ask the children to tell you the places they have seen water—lakes, rivers, a swimming pool, the ocean. Accept all responses.

2. With the children, pretend to swim through water, making big arm motions and pretending to come up for air.

3. Crouch down with the children; then, tell them that when the sun shines, it turns the water into vapor that goes up into the clouds. Slowly rise up to the sky and reach up, up, up!

4. Tell them that the rain falls down, down, down from the clouds. Slowly trickle back down to the floor like raindrops falling from a cloud.

5. Tell the children that the water flows back into the rivers, lakes, and oceans. Pretend to swim through water again.

6. Tell the children that plants and animals need to drink water. Encourage the children to show how animals or plants drink water.

7. Tell the children that people need water, too, to stay healthy. Ask the children to pretend to drink water.

8. Ask them where they can get good, clean water to drink:
    - from the water faucet (Pretend to turn on a faucet.)
    - from a water fountain (Pretend to drink from a fountain.)
    - from a bottle (Pretend to fill a water bottle and drink from it.)

9. Say, "I'm thirsty from all this talk about water. Let's get some real water now!" Take the children to the water fountain or fill a pitcher with water and pour into cups for all.

Even very young children can have a basic understanding of the water cycle:
- Rainwater falls down, down, down from clouds.
- The water falls on plants and animals and people, who drink it up.
- The water collects in big lakes, flowing rivers, and deep oceans.
- The sun shines brightly and turns the water back into a vapor.
- The water vapor goes up, up, up into the air where it collects as clouds.

Pumpkin Patch

Use this imaginative activity to support children's learning about how pumpkins grow and how they are used.

How to Do It

1. Gather the children together and ask them if they know what a pumpkin is. Listen as the children describe pumpkins. If possible, provide a real pumpkin for the children to examine.
2. Tell the children, "Today, we are all going to be pumpkins. Spread out around the room on the floor to make a pumpkin patch!"
3. Ask, "How would you become a little seed in the patch?" Crouch down and roll into a ball like a seed.
4. Explain, "We pumpkins grow from the seeds, starting small and then growing bigger and bigger on our vines. Show me how you grow to a small pumpkin."
5. Say, "Now show me how you grow bigger and rounder." Encourage the children to pretend to be pumpkins growing larger.
6. Say, "Now let's jump up and pretend to be the people who are coming to pick the pumpkins! We are walking through the patch. Which pumpkin do we want to bring home? Look around to choose one. When you find one, pick it up and carry it. Skip around and have some fun! Skip around while carrying your pumpkin!"
7. Ask, "When you take your pumpkin home, what will you use it for?" Listen as the children tell you how they will use their pumpkins: pumpkin pie, dried pumpkin seeds, or a special carving for a holiday.

Expand It!

Toast pumpkin seeds to share with the children.

The Fruit Tree Story

Support children's understanding that some yummy fruits grow on trees.

How to Do It

1. Ask the children to name some fruits that grow on trees. If they are not sure, suggest a few: apples, pears, peaches, plums, or any fruits that grow in your area. If possible, show the children pictures of these trees, or offer the real fruit for them to examine.
2. Tell them, "We are going to pretend to go apple picking!" (Or name any fruit that is available in your area.)
3. Ask the children to stand up and spread out. Say, "We climb and climb up the big, big tree." Encourage the children to pretend to climb up a tree using big arm and leg motions.
4. Ask, "We're at the top—what do we see? Pretend to look around. Say, "Apples for you and you!" Everyone jump for joy!
5. Pretend to gather all the apples on the tree, reaching way up high and bend low to put the apples in your basket.
6. Say, "Okay, now we're finished! Let's climb down!" Pretend to climb back down the tree, using big arm and leg motions.
7. Invite the children to sit down and count their apples with you. "Let's count our apples: one, two, three!"

Expand It!

Serve fruits that grow on trees for snacktime or lunch.

What Does Food Feel Like?

Teaching children about different food textures can help them distinguish among foods and may encourage them to try new foods.

How to Do It

1. Gather examples of different foods to show the children. If you cannot bring in real examples for the children to explore, you can use photos. If you decide to use photos, ask the children what they think the real food might feel like.

2. Ask the children to sit in a circle. Hold up an example or picture of a food (for example, broccoli, pasta, avocado, apple, corn, blueberry, or string cheese). Let the children touch the food if they wish and describe it. If you're using photos, ask the children to tell you what they think the food might feel like. (Some children will have prior experience with a particular food. If so, let them tell you what the food feels like.)

3. Invite the children to act how they think the food feels to touch. For example, show them a picture of broccoli. Ask them to show you with their bodies what broccoli feels like. The children may jump up and down with small, bumpy arm movements. Or, they may stand up straight and tall and hold their arms over their heads. However they choose to interpret broccoli is fine.

4. Continue with other foods and ask the children to show you with their body movements how they think those foods feel to the touch. For pasta, they may make whole-body wave movements. For carrot, they may use stiff arms and legs while moving around. The children can crouch down all together, and then you can come and "pull" them out of the ground.

Expand It!

Gather foods and put them into boxes with small openings. Have the children feel the foods and describe how each one feels (bumpy, smooth, stiff, and so on). Ask them to guess what foods could be in the boxes. If they wish, let the children try the (washed!) foods to find out what the foods taste like.

I Can Be a Role Model

Support a healthy self-image and self-esteem as you teach the children that they can be role models for healthy eating.

How to Do It

1. Ask the children what a healthy lunch might consist of. Listen to their responses. If they offer suggestions for processed foods, encourage them to think about healthier alternatives. Tell them that they can be role models for healthy eating. That means they can show their brothers, sisters, cousins, and friends how to eat healthy foods.

2. Tell them, "For lunch, I like to eat a sandwich and maybe some soup. For dessert, I like to have apples." Pretend to set out a healthy lunch:

   I have my sandwich here. (Pretend to hold a sandwich.)

   It's a _____ sandwich. (Name a healthy sandwich you like.)

   And here is my bowl of soup. (Pretend to set out a bowl of soup and a spoon.)

   For dessert I have an apple. (Pretend to hold and admire an apple.)

3. Invite the children to make a lunch with you:

   Now let's try making a sandwich like mine! (Mime making a sandwich, filling it with healthy ingredients. Pretend to eat it all up.)

   I'm going to eat my vegetable soup. (Pretend to spoon soup and eat it.)

   Vegetables give us vitamins and keep us strong.

   Can you help me chop my fresh green apple? (Pretend to chop an apple with a simple hand rhythm.)

   Apples give us energy and keep us healthy. (Pretend to eat slices.)

4. Encourage the children to volunteer to lead the class in making a healthy pretend lunch. Ask each volunteer to name one healthy food and to lead the class in "making" it.

5. Ask the children to tell you who they might be a role model for in encouraging healthy eating.

Expand It!

Consider sharing a healthy snack at snacktime with a younger class.

Be a good role model for the children. Bring in healthy foods to eat for lunch and snack so they can see you enjoying good nutrition. Talk about the foods you eat, and encourage the children to try healthy foods at home.

I Like to Eat This!

Use peer modeling to encourage children to try new healthy foods. Children are more likely to try a new food when they see a peer choosing and eating it.

How to Do It

1. Ask the children to sit in a circle or at a table, and ask for a volunteer to help you lead the exercise.
2. Ask the child to name a healthy food that she likes to eat. If she has trouble thinking of a healthy food, suggest one that you have observed her enjoying or have heard her make positive comments about.
3. Lead the child in a short discussion about foods she likes:
   - What's a healthy food that you like to eat?
   - What does this food look like? Show us the shape! (Encourage the child to make a shape of the food with her hands or body, and encourage the other children to make that shape.)
   - What color is it?
   - What does it feel like? Is it hard, or is it soft?
   - Is it crunchy or quiet when you eat it?
   - How does it taste?
   - How do you like to eat this food at home? Do you like to eat it plain or with other foods, too?
4. Invite the children to pretend to cut up this food and eat it with the volunteer.
5. Ask for another volunteer to talk about a healthy food he likes to eat. Continue in this manner as long as the children are interested.

Expand It!

If possible, have some healthy foods ready to try for a snack. Invite the children to help cut and serve the foods.

At Home, We Like to Eat This!

Celebrate cultural preferences and the home environment while using peer modeling to encourage children to try new healthy foods.

How to Do It

Note: *Before doing this activity, it may be helpful to ask families for examples of healthy foods they enjoy at home, in case the children cannot remember foods to name.*

1. Ask the children to sit in a circle or at a table, and ask for a volunteer to help you lead the exercise.
2. Ask the child to name a healthy food that he likes to eat at home with his family.
3. Lead the child in a short discussion of a food he enjoys at home:
   - What is a food you like to eat at home with your family?
   - What does this food look like? Show us the shape! (Encourage the child to make a shape of the food with his hands or body, and encourage the other children to make that shape.)
   - What color is it?
   - What does it feel like? Is it hard, or is it soft?
   - Is it crunchy or quiet when you eat it?
   - How does it taste?
   - How do you like to eat this food at home? Do you like to eat it plain or with other foods too?
4. Invite the children to pretend to make the food with the child. Ask the child to tell the group how he or a family member makes that food. If the child has difficulty remembering, ask a few questions that will help him tell the class how to make the dish.
   - How do we mix it up or chop it up?
   - Do we cook it?
   - How do we eat it?

   Young children's explanations of cooking can be quite funny. Listen respectfully and consider sharing the child's explanation with his family.
5. Ask for another volunteer to talk about a healthy food she likes to eat with her family. Continue in this manner as long as the children are interested.

Expand It!

If possible and if your facility allows, consider asking families to provide dishes for the children to sample. Be sure to get a recipe for each dish to check for possible food allergens. If you are unable to bring in real samples, consider providing photos of the foods.

My Name Is _____, and This Is What I Make

Encourage self-esteem and healthy food decision making with this fun, catchy chant.

How to Do It

1. Invite the children to sit cross-legged with you in a big circle. Teach the children the following chant as you clap a rhythm together:

   My name is Susan, and this is what I make! Salad! (Susan stands in the center of the circle and mimes making a salad.)

   My name is Billy, and this is what I make! Chili! (Billy stands in the center of the circle and mimes making chili.)

2. Encourage the children to name healthy foods that they enjoy eating. If they have trouble thinking of examples, you might suggest the following:

   - Chicken
   - Carrots
   - Peas
   - Broccoli
   - Asparagus
   - Pasta
   - Mashed Potatoes
   - Fish
   - Tomatoes
   - Peaches
   - Cherries
   - Raspberries
   - Smoothies
   - Eggs
   - Cashews

3. Continue clapping and chanting until everyone has had a turn. Applaud yourselves for eating healthy foods!

Expand It!

Make a restaurant in the dramatic play center, where each child can pretend to make and serve his food to the other children.

In a Hurry—Here's a Store!

While we realize that children need a healthy breakfast, it is a sad reality that busy parents and caregivers sometimes give children food purchased in convenience stores. Teach the children they can ask for healthy choices—even on the run.

How to Do It

Note: *Before you do this exercise, make sure all the children have had breakfast; have breakfast foods available just in case. In the dramatic play area or scattered around the room, place cutouts of photographs of healthy foods commonly found in convenience stores. Or, consider placing clean, empty food containers around the room.*

1. Gather the children together. Encourage them to mime leaving the house in morning, opening and closing the door. Pretend to run out of the house and around the room.
2. Say, "Wait! We haven't had breakfast, but we are already outside. We're in a hurry! Here's a store! What can we find here for breakfast?"
3. Discuss what might be some good choices that can be found at a convenience store: yogurt, wheat cereal and milk, fruit, or a whole-wheat roll. If possible, hold up empty food containers or photographs of healthy foods, so the children will be able to recognize them.
4. Say, "Okay, find them in the store." Encourage the children to look for the healthy food choices in the dramatic play area or around the room.
5. Say, "Okay, let's bring the foods to the counter." Encourage the children to run around again, pretending to carry foods and put them on counter.
6. Say, "Now let's eat them up!" Encourage the children to pretend to eat.
7. Say, "Let's go to school!" Encourage the children to run to school. Mime opening the door and closing the door. "Come on in and find your seats in the circle." Guide the children to find a seat in the circle.

Expand It!

- Do the same exercise with healthy lunch foods, such as sandwiches on whole-wheat bread, fruit, yogurt, milk, and cheese.
- Consider offering healthy foods such as yogurt, fruit, and whole-wheat rolls to taste during snack time.

Five Healthy Choices

Fast-food restaurants and children's menus often offer foods that are not the healthiest choices for children. Use this activity to teach children that they can make healthy choices in restaurants.

How to Do It

1. Before doing this exercise with the children, make a simple picture menu using cutouts of photographs of foods commonly found in fast-food restaurants or on children's menus. Be sure to include to healthy choices and some not-so-healthy choices.

2. Invite the children to sit with you on the circle-time rug. Say, "Let's pretend that we are in a restaurant." Ask the children to name a restaurant that you can pretend to visit.

3. Ask, "What happens when you go to a restaurant?" Encourage the children to tell you what happens in a restaurant: the customer looks at a menu, a waiter or cashier takes the order, a cook prepares the food, the waiter or cashier gives the food to the customer.

4. Say, "This is the menu for our pretend restaurant. What do we have to choose from?" Go over the menu with the children.

5. Ask, "What will we choose for our lunch in our pretend restaurant?" Listen to the children's suggestions. Ask, "Are these healthy food choices?" Discuss what healthy choices can be in a restaurant. Guide children to some healthy food and drink choices, such as the following examples:
   - Protein and Grain—roast beef sandwich, grilled chicken drumstick, plain hamburger
   - Vegetable—carrot sticks or corn
   - Fruit—apple slices
   - Drink—plain skim or 1% milk or water

6. Guide the children through ordering food. "Let's help order our food. Ready? Let's say our list together. 'May I please have (healthy choices, such as a plain hamburger, carrot sticks, apple slices, and milk).'" Repeat this a few times to give the children some practice.

7. Pretend to pick up your food from the counter. "We said *please* when we ordered. What do we say now?" Listen to the children's suggestions. "Right! *Thank you*. Let's say it together: Thank you! Okay, let's pretend to eat our food."

Expand It!

In the home living or dramatic play area, encourage the children to create their own restaurant. Ask the children what healthy foods they could serve in their restaurant.

No, No—That Doesn't Go! Yes, Yes—That Is Best!

This exercise uses young children's love of the word *no* to encourage them to make healthy food choices.

How to Do It

1. Gather the children to sit with you. Talk with them about what makes a healthy dinner. Offer different food suggestions, and encourage them to say whether or not that choice is a healthy one.

2. Say, "We are going to pretend to make a big dinner. What shall we start with?" Listen as the children offer their ideas. Then say, "How about some wiggly pasta? Let's all stand up and become wiggly pasta. I see pasta!" Stand up with them and make wiggly body movements. "Pour on the sauce!" Pretend to pour sauce into wiggly pasta.

3. Suggest another dish, such as turkey meatballs. "Let's add turkey meatballs! Make a shape of a ball." Pretend to make turkey meatballs and put them with the pasta.

4. Continue in this manner, occasionally suggesting a silly or unhealthy food such as worms or cake or tree branches or cars. When you make a silly suggestion, encourage the children to say, "No! No! That doesn't go!" Encourage the children to offer their ideas of healthy dishes to have for dinner and to mime putting the foods on the plate, saying "Yes! Yes! That is best!" If they cannot think of a healthy food, suggest some, such as peas or carrots.

5. Say, "Wow! We have made a lot of food! Have we made healthy choices? Yes! Yes! That is best!"

6. Ask the children to suggest a drink to go with dinner. Encourage them to mime holding cups. Suggest a really big cup of cola. Ask the children if that would be a healthy choice. Lead them to the understanding that cola has too much sugar. "No! No! That doesn't go!" Ask them to suggest healthier alternatives, such as milk or water. "Yes! Yes! That is best!" Pretend to pour the milk or water in their cups.

7. Pretend to eat your healthy dinner. Then say, "Wow! I ate a lot! How about you? We ate our pasta with turkey meatballs and sauce and yummy peas and carrots. Yes! Yes! That is best!"

Filling Grandma's Grocery Cart

Support children in learning to recognize and select healthy foods at the grocery store.

How to Do It

1. Ask the children if they have ever been to a grocery store with a family member. Listen to their responses. Ask them what types of foods they remember seeing.

2. Tell them that today you will pretend to be shopping with Grandma. You will help her select healthy foods for the family. Stand and pretend to push a grocery cart. Ask the children to do the same. Encourage the children to push the carts up one way and down another, three or four times, to get used to the fun of the pretend cart.

3. Gather the children and walk through the classroom, pretending to walk down the aisles of a market. Explain that each line you travel in a store is called an aisle or section. "Grandma says she wants you to help her put healthy foods in her basket. She wants to bring the food home, make a nice dinner, and have some food left for a good snack. Let's go!"

4. Say, "First let's go in the store to the fruit section. I see lots of bins and shelves of fruit! What fruits do you see?" Let the children name some fruits and pretend to put them in their baskets. "Grandma says she sees apples, grapes, bananas, papayas, oranges, avocados, peaches, pears, and pineapple. She wants to make fruit salad and some fresh fruit juice." Pretend to put a few of these into your basket, naming the selections.

5. Say, "Now let's turn into the vegetable aisle. I see lots of bins and shelves of vegetables! What do you see?" Let the children name vegetables and select some to put in their baskets. "Grandma says she sees cucumber, lettuce, carrots, celery, bell pepper, eggplant, broccoli, sweet potato, tomato, and a nice big pumpkin. She wants to make vegetable soup and a salad." Name your selections as you put them in your cart.

6. Continue in this manner, shopping with the children in each section and naming foods you can make with the selections:
   - Protein section: chicken, beef, fish, nuts, and beans (chicken soup, shish kebabs, grilled fish, nut butter, beans)
   - Dairy section: milk, cheese, and yogurt

- Grains section: pasta, rice, bulgur wheat, quinoa, and wheat flour (pasta, rice, tabouli, quinoa salad, rolls)

7. Say, "Let's go to the bread aisle last and get some crackers for our snack and some bread for tomorrow, too! Grandma wants to go home and make us a snack!" Pretend to wheel your carts to the checkout counter and help Grandma take everything out of the cart and put it on the counter. Pretend to help put the food in the grocery bags and carry everything home.

Expand It!

- For a longer activity, add Grandma's Chicken Soup to the end of the exercise.
- Consider providing samples of one or more foods from each section for the children to try.
- Create a grocery store in the dramatic play area.

What's in Your Basket?

Do this brief stretching exercise to help the children settle down and focus.

How to Do It

1. Ask the children to lie on their stomachs in a big circle. Tell them that they are going to make baskets with their bodies. Encourage them to bend their knees and reach back to grab their ankles, performing a basket stretch. While they hold their ankles, make sure they are facing forward in order not to strain their necks. Alternatively, this exercise can be done with a table stretch. Begin seated on bottoms with hands behind backs, and lift bottoms off the floor to make bodies parallel with the floor. Ask, "What food is on your table?"

2. Take turns asking each student, "What food is in your basket (or on your table)? Make it something healthy." Encourage the children to name healthy foods.

3. Relax and breathe in and out.

Head to Toe, Letter O; These Are Foods that Make Me Grow

This fun little rhyme will teach children which foods are healthy for them!

How to Do It

1. Teach the children the following rhyme and motions. Do this together as a group until the children can do it on their own. Then, individual children can volunteer to be the leader and take turns leading the group.

   Head (Arms high)

   To toe (Touch toes)

   Letter *O* (Make the shape of an *O* with hands)

   These are foods that help me grow! (Move head and twist side to side)

   (Child calls out the name of a healthy food.)

2. Consider offering pictures of different healthy foods that the children might call out:
   - Protein: fish, beans, yogurt
   - Grain: brown rice, quinoa, barley
   - Vegetables: carrots, brussel sprouts, corn
   - Fruit: mango, apple, strawberry

Expand It!

Chant this during wait times to help keep the children focused and occupied.

Good-for-You Foods

This activity helps children learn how certain foods are healthy for specific body parts.

How to Do It

1. Before beginning, gather photos of each food you will discuss. Consider bringing in samples of the real foods for the children to explore and taste.
2. Ask the children to stand with enough room around them to wiggle about.
3. Tell them they are going to learn about foods that help certain parts of their bodies. As they learn about each food, they can move to show how that body part might move when it gets the yummy food. For example, when you show them broccoli, which looks like a tree and helps them stay healthy like a tree, they can stand tall like a strong, healthy tree.
4. As you hold up a photo or real example of each food, tell them what that food looks like to help them remember the body part that the food is good for.

Food	Looks Like	Why it is good for you!
Broccoli	A tree (florets are leaves)	Makes you stay healthy like a big tree
Celery	A long, straight bone	Makes your bones strong
Walnut	A brain, squiggly with two halves	Makes your brain grow
Carrot	An eye (round when cut)	Makes your eyes see well
Tomato	A heart (chambers and color)	Makes your heart strong
Ginger	A stomach (same shape)	Takes away tummy aches

Expand It!

Put the vegetables in a bag or box. Have children touch them without seeing them to guess what they might be. Then show them the vegetable.

Food Dance!

This activity is a silly way to encourage children to think about healthy eating.

How to Do It

1. Ask the children to stand in a circle. Tell the children that you will call out a specific food, and they are to make their bodies in the shape of that food and dance around like they think that food would dance.
2. Call out a variety of foods such as the following. Some are easier than others, so accept any of the children's attempts to make those shapes and dance around. (Prepare to giggle!):
   - Banana
   - Tomato
   - Spaghetti
   - Turkey
3. Let the children call out foods for the rest of the class to imitate.

The Energy Timer

Help children understand which foods give us long-lasting energy and which give us only short-term energy.

How to Do It

1. Gather the children on one side of the room and tell them they will travel along a line, the Energy Line. Tell them that some foods give lots of energy and will let them go all the way up the line and back, and some just will not.

2. Start with healthy foods that will give the energy to go all the way up the line and back. "How about sweet potatoes? They help us go far!" Encourage the children to walk several steps away, then turn and run back.

3. Suggest a sugary, unhealthy food. "What about candy? That won't take us very far!" Stop the children after only a few steps and tell them to come back.

4. Continue in this manner, suggesting both healthy and unhealthy foods:
   - Healthy: Proteins such as turkey, nuts, or beans
   - Unhealthy: Junk food such as potato chips
   - Healthy: Vegetables and fruits such as carrots and bananas

5. Encourage the children to call out different foods, and tell them how far they will go on those foods.

Expand It!

Encourage the children to skip, hop, or gallop up the Energy Line and back.

Knock-Knock! Nutrition!

Children love knock-knock jokes. Have fun making up silly jokes that reinforce learning the names of healthy foods.

How to Do It

1. Ask the children if they know what a knock-knock joke is. Tell them that this is a joke where you pretend to knock on a door and then say a silly line when the other person pretends to answer.

2. Offer an example such as the following:

   Teacher: *Knock! Knock!* (Knock on the pretend door two times)
   Children: *Who's there?* (Jump back one time to listen)
   Teacher: *Banana!* (Make body in the shape of a banana)
   Children: *Banana who?* (Make bodies in the shape of bananas)
   Teacher: *Knock! Knock!* (Knock on the pretend door two times)
   Children: *Who's there?* (Jump back one time to listen)
   Teacher: *Banana!* (Make body in the shape of a banana)
   Children: *Banana who?* (Make bodies in the shape of bananas)
   Teacher: *Knock! Knock!* (Knock on the pretend door two times)
   Children: *Who's there?* (Jump back one time to listen)
   Teacher: *Orange!* (Make the shape of an orange with hands)
   Children: *Orange who?* (Make the shape of an orange with hands)
   Teacher: *Orange you glad I didn't say banana?* (Shake head side to side)

3. Continue with other knock-knock jokes, acting them out with the children:

   - Who's there? Bean. Bean who? Bean a long time that I've been waiting here!
   - Who's there? Olive. Olive who? Olive you so very much!
   - Who's there? Pear. Pear who? I see a pear of shoes over here!
   - Who's there? Squash. Squash who? Don't squash me when you open the door!

Let's Pack a Snack!

Teach children about healthy choices for a snack.

How to Do It

1. Teach the children the following chant:

   Snack (clap, jump)

   Pack (clap, jump)

   Let's Pack (Reach forward with two hands as if holding a baggie.)

   A Snack (Pull back with hands)

   What are we going to pack today?

   Let's pack some fruit! (say the name of any healthy fruit)

2. Each time you do the chant with the children, encourage them to run to the other side of the room and mime getting that snack item and bringing it back to the line.

3. Continue in this manner, letting the children suggest healthy snacks.

Mama's Little Baby Likes

Sing a fun song as you act out eating healthy foods. This song is great for transitions or wait times!

How to Do It

1. Stand in a circle with the children. Teach them the following song, sung to the tune of "Shortnin' Bread":
    Mama's little baby likes corn, corn (Sway side-to-side, pretending to hold corn and stepping toward the center of the circle.)
    Mamma's little baby likes to eat corn (Pretend to take a bite)
    Step back Sally,
    Step back Sally,
    Step back Sally (Step backward six times)
    Crunch! Crunch! Crunch! (Stamp feet)
    Eating corn! (Hold up arms and hands, as if holding an ear of corn.)
2. Continue singing, saying the names of healthy foods such as beans, squash, peaches, plums, milk, cheese, bread, rice, and so on. Make up an action to go with each type of food.
3. Ask the children to suggest a healthy food to sing about, and make up an action to go with it.

Expand It!

Eat some of the foods you sing about at snack or lunchtime.

ABCs of Fruits and Veggies

Connect alphabet learning with learning the names of fruits and vegetables. Do this activity as a group, and then let the students take turns and pick the letter they want to be.

How to Do It

1. Before beginning, consider posting the alphabet poem below on a whiteboard or a large piece of paper.

2. Ask the children to sit in a circle, and ask them to name a fruit or vegetable that begins with the letter *A* (or the letter your class is learning). Give the children time to offer their ideas, and write the ideas on a whiteboard, a chart, or on a piece of paper. Ask them if they have eaten any of these foods. Did they like them? Accept all responses.

3. Tell the children that they will learn a rhyme using the alphabet and the names of fruits and vegetables.

4. Teach the children the following poem. For each type of food, encourage them to stand and form a shape with their bodies that they think is the shape of that food, or encourage them to move like they think that food would move. If the children do not know what a particular food looks like, describe it for them.
   Note: You may want to break the poem into smaller parts and do it over several days.
   A is for apple, *B* is for beet,
   C is for cantaloupe, down near my feet.
   D is for date, *E* is for eggplant,
   F is for fig—makes me get up and jig!
   G is for grapefruit, high up in the tree.
   H is for ham—gives protein that makes me what I am!
   I is for ice pop, *J* is for jackfruit,
   K is for kale, makes me run fast like a tiger with a tail!
   L is for lime, *M* is for melon,
   N is for nuts, no ifs, ands, or buts!
   O is for okra, *P* is for pineapple, *Q* is for quinoa,
   R is for raspberry—I love a good berry.
   S is for spinach, *T* is for turnip,
   U is for udon, a noodle that looks like a poodle!

V is for vegetable, *W* is for watermelon,

X is for xia*, Chinese for *shrimp*.

Y is for yucca,

Z is for zucchini, inside it's slippery like linguini and fettuccini!

Expand It!

Have some of these foods for lunch or snack.

Xia is pronounced /shah/.

Vegetable Wall Chart and Song

Encourage the children to try new vegetables and keep a record of their reactions to these new foods.

How to Do It

1. Create a simple chart that lists the names of the children down one side and the names and pictures of common vegetables across the top columns. Post it in the classroom where the children can reach it and refer to it.

2. Encourage and help the children to put a mark next to their names in the appropriate column when they try a new vegetable. This can be done in a couple of ways, either by reviewing vegetables that the children have tried in the past few days, or by offering a vegetable during class lunchtime or snack.
   - Make a check mark if they liked the vegetable.
   - Make an O if they thought the vegetable was so-so.
   - Make an X if they did not like the vegetable at all.

3. On a regular basis—daily or weekly—review the chart with the children. Teach children the following vegetable song to sing before you review the veggie adventures with them:

   Sung to the tune of "Mary Had a Little Lamb"

   Today we ate a vegetable, vegetable, vegetable (Clapping hands)

   Today we ate a vegetable

   and this is how I liked it.

   Today we ate some carrots, carrots, carrots (Vary the vegetable you sing about;)

   Today we ate some carrots (Make shape of that vegetable with the body)

   And this is how I liked it. (Arms out to sides)

   Today I really liked it, liked it, liked it (Make happy face and wiggle around)

   Or maybe just a little bit, (Make "so-so" face, shrugging shoulders)

   Or really not at all! (Frown and shake head)

   If today I don't like it, like it, like it (Shake head and body no)

   Tomorrow I might like it

   A little bit more (Nod head and body yes)

   And mark it on the wall! (Make a check mark motion with arm and hand while standing on tiptoe)

4. If you choose to ask the children about the vegetables they have tried on their own, ask for volunteers to come up and make a mark to show what vegetables they tried and how they liked them. If you choose to do this activity when the whole class tries a vegetable, ask for volunteers to come up to mark how they liked that vegetable. Any response (like, dislike, or not sure) is appropriate and acceptable. The important thing is to encourage the children to try new foods.

5. Review the chart with the children to find out which vegetables are most liked, which are least liked, and which ones the children are not sure about yet. Remind them that even if they do not like a vegetable the first time, they may like it later on.

Expand It!

As an alternative, you may wish to have the children make individual Vegetable Charts on which to record their culinary adventures.

The Greenies

Support good self-esteem as you teach the children what greens are and why they are good for us.

How to Do It

1. Ask the children if they can name some green vegetables. If they run out of examples, suggest peas, zucchini, broccoli, lettuce, asparagus, green beans, kale, collard greens, spinach, or green peppers.
2. Tell the children that green vegetables have lots of vitamins and help to make children superhero strong.
3. Tell them that they are going to make their bodies superhero strong by being Greeny Guys and Greeny Girls. Ask them to think about what vegetables they could use to make your strong Greeny body:
   - Strong legs might be made of zucchini and asparagus.
   - Strong arms may be made of spinach.
   - Superhero fingers and hands might be made of green peppers.
   - Superhero Greeny feet and toes could be made of peas and green beans.
   - Superhero tummies may be made of kale.
   - Super-smart brains might be made of broccoli.

   Let the children name the green vegetables they like and want their bodies to be made of.
4. Encourage them to put on their super capes and fly around.

Parachute Tossed Salad

Teach the children about making a salad, what they can put into it, and why a salad is a healthy choice to make.

How to Do It

1. This activity may be done with or without an actual parachute.
2. Ask the children to stand in a circle. Explain to them that they will be making a Parachute Tossed Salad, tossing the vegetables that make up a salad into the "salad bowl" in the middle of the circle.
3. Ask them to grasp the handles of the parachute (real or imaginary) and go around and around in a circle in a variety of gaits:
    - Baby steps
    - Giant steps
    - Gallop
    - Jump
    - Skip (for older children)

    First go in one direction, and then stop and go the other way. Put down the parachute.
4. Call out a salad fixing; for example, lettuce. Ask the children to pretend to chop up the lettuce with their hands and then toss the lettuce into the salad bowl with big arm actions.
5. Pick up the parachute again and toss the lettuce up and down. Put down the parachute.
6. Continue in this manner, calling out ingredients to add to the salad, chopping or washing them, and then tossing them into the bowl.
7. Add a little salad dressing just before you're done! Use olive oil (you can stomp the olives to get the oil, if you want) and vinegar, mixing them together and pouring them in.

Expand It!

Let the children help you make a real tossed salad to try at lunchtime.

Do the Dip!

Encourage children to try new vegetables dipped into healthy dips such as plain low-fat or nonfat yogurt, low-fat mayonnaise, reduced-fat cream cheese, or hummus.

How to Do It

1. Ask the children to stand in a circle. Explain to them they are making the shape of a dipping bowl, and you will all be choosing different vegetables to pretend to dip into the bowl.
2. Name the kind of dip that will be in the center of the circle. Start with yogurt. Have children pretend to pour the dip into the center with big arm actions, then use a giant spoon and stir it up.
3. Call out the name of a vegetable (you may also show a picture of it, or hold up the actual vegetable), and encourage the children to make the shape of that vegetable with their bodies.
4. Say, "Let's dip the vegetable in the dip. Do the dip!" Encourage the children to raise their arms high above their heads and pretend to dip by bending over toward the center of the circle and then standing back up. Repeat three times: count one, dip and stand up; two, dip and stand up; three, dip and stand up.
5. Pretend to eat the vegetable. "Crunch, crunch, crunch. Yum, that is good!"
6. Name another vegetable, and do the dip again!

Expand It!

-   If possible, offer the children real vegetables and dip to try.
-   Encourage them to try new fruits by dipping them into low-fat or nonfat yogurt mixed with honey and a little orange juice.

Turn your home living center or dramatic play area into a fruit stand. Ask the children to decide which fruits to sell, and help them set up an area where they can pretend to buy, sell, prepare, and eat yummy fruits. Make signs, giving the name of the store and listing the fruits and the prices, to post in the area.

Melting Fruit Pops

Yummy fruit makes a wonderful frozen dessert. Children develop their motor skills as they pretend to freeze and melt.

How to Do It

1. Tell the children that they are going to pretend to be frozen fruit pops. Say, "Oh, it's a hot day! Let's make some frozen fruit pops."
2. Ask the children to sit in a circle. Decide on a fruit to make into a fruit pop.
3. Pretend to pick the fruit, cut it up, and put it in ice-pop molds.
4. Say, "Now, we need to pour in some fruit juice." Walk around the room and pretend to pour 100 percent fruit juice on the children as if they were the ice cube tray.
5. Pretend the room gets very cold, and the children are the fruit in the ice pop molds in the freezer. Say, "The freezer is a very cold place, so all the fruit and juice froze very fast into a fruit pop! Let me see you frozen!" Encourage the children to hug their knees, pretending to be frozen solid like a fruit pop.
6. Pretend to take the fruit pops out of the freezer. Say, "It's such a hot day! I took the fruit pops out of the freezer, and they are starting to melt right away! Melting, melting, melting into a puddle!"
7. Encourage the children to melt slowly, lying on their backs on the floor with their arms and legs stretched out.
8. Pretend to put the fruit pops back into the freezer, saying, "Oh, back in the freezer! Let me see you frozen again!" The children slowly tuck their chins, lift their bodies up, and hug their knees in tight, frozen like a fruit pop again.
9. Have fun pretending to put the fruit pops in and out of the freezer, pretending to melt and freeze.

Expand It!

Make fruit pops with the children, using fresh fruit and 100 percent fruit juice or water. Have these yummy fruit pops for a snack.

Fruit Rap

Do this silly chant with the children, then learn about making fruit leather.

How to Do It

1. Ask the children to stand in a circle.
2. Teach them the following rap, clapping on the repeated words:

   Apple, apple, apple, apple, apple, apple, ORANGE! (make body into shape of orange, round shape)

   Grape, grape, grape, grape, grape, grape, BANANA! (make body into a long banana shape)

   Berry, berry, berry, berry, berry, berry, SILLY! (wiggle all around)

   Mash it all up and make a fruit wrap! (jump up and down to mash the fruit with their feet)

   Wrap it all up! (Children hug themselves and spin around three times)

   That's a wrap!

Expand It!

Consider making fruit leather with the children to share at snack time.

Fruit Salad Fun

Children love to eat sweet fruits. Teach them about different fruits, and let the children pretend to make a delicious and healthy fruit salad.

How to Do It

1. Pretend to be in a garden. Ask the children if they see any fruits. If a child says she sees an apple, say, "Oh yes! Apples are juicy and sweet. Let's pick some from this tree!"
2. Pretend to pick the fruits chosen by children from the trees, bushes, and so on, and pretend to place the fruits in baskets. If the children do not know many types of fruits, offer some suggestions: peach, pear, apple, blueberry, raspberry, pineapple, guava, strawberry, orange, tangerine, cherry, plum, date, fig, banana, cantaloupe, grapefruit, grapes, kiwi, and mango. You can also add fruits that are seasonal or fruits that are sold locally. Consider providing photos of the fruits, so the children can see what they look like.
3. Gather the children in a circle, and pretend to wash and chop the fruits.
4. Pretend to toss the fruit into a bowl (the middle of the circle) using big arm motions.
5. Mix the fruit salad using spoons (arms) and big arm motions.
6. Jump around in the middle of the circle to mix up the fruit even more.
7. Have children individually pretend to take some fruit and put it into a little bowl and pretend to eat up the fruit.

Expand It!

Make an actual fruit salad to eat. Let the children choose the fruits they want to include, and let them help wash, add, and stir the fruits.

Grandma's Chicken Soup

This activity helps children connect turning healthy ingredients into something yummy by cooking.

How to Do It

1. Gather the children around you, and ask them if they eat soup at home. Ask them if they can explain how to make soup. Listen to their responses; you should get some pretty interesting answers.

2. Tell them you are going to pretend to make chicken soup. Ask them to show you how they pretend to get the ingredients from the refrigerator. First, ask them to pretend to take out the following: chicken, barley, celery, carrot, onion, and garlic. Put each item on a counter.

3. Make a circle and pretend to have a big pot in the center of the circle. Ask them to pretend to get a pitcher and to pour water in the pot.

4. Ask them to pretend to chop up their ingredients, beginning with the chicken, as you count 1–2–3–4, 1–2–3–4; then, put the ingredient into the pot.

5. Next, ask them to chop up the celery and carrot, using a faster rhythm, doubling the beats, 1–2, 1–2, and tossing the pieces into the pot.

6. Chop the garlic and onion (they can pretend to cry from the onion) and triple the chopping rhythm, 1–2–3, 1–2–3, and toss the pieces into the pot. Toss in some barley, too.

7. Tell them to take a big spoon and stir the soup round and round. Do this as a group and then give each child a turn. While waiting for each child to stir, talk about the protein, vegetables, and grain that will make this soup taste good, and how cooking it changes the taste and texture of each ingredient.

8. Pretend the soup is cooking, and talk about how the ingredients are getting softer and their tastes are mixing into the water to give it the chicken soup its delicious taste.

9. Say, "It is finished cooking!" Pretend to ladle a serving in a little bowl for each child. Eat the soup and talk about how it tastes. Each child can say what he or she likes about the soup.

Expand It!

If possible, repeat the exercise by actually making a chicken soup in the classroom. Have prechopped ingredients ready, and let the children put each ingredient into the pot. Let each child take a turn pouring some water into the pot from a pitcher. As they work, ask the children to identify the ingredients. Let them take turns stirring the pot. Take the soup to a kitchen to cook it, and return with soup to serve at snack or lunch the next day.

This activity can be paired with "What Do We Put in Grandma's Grocery Cart?" on page 36.

The Protein Chant

Teach children where protein comes from, what it does, and why it is an important part of a healthy diet.

How to Do It

1. Teach the children the following chant. Teach the words first, while the children are sitting, and then stand up in place for the exercise:

    (To the cadence of the army marching chant "I Don't Know, but I've Been Told")

    Protein makes my muscles strong, (Make a muscle with one arm and then both arms)

    Gives me energy all day long. (Pump arms in the air, alternating arms)

    I like protein, (clap, clap)

    What is protein? (clap, clap)

    Helps me grow, (Squat and then stand up)

    Helps me know, (Point to head with one hand)

    Helps me think, (Point to head with two hands)

    Helps me blink. (Blink twice while "blinking" fingers open and closed, too)

    I like protein, (clap, clap)

    That is protein! (clap, clap)

2. To help children understand where protein is found, replace the word *protein* with the words *meat, beans, peas, fish, chicken, soybeans, milk, nuts, eggs,* and *cheese.* You can use all of these words in one exercise, or you can choose a few words to do each time you do this exercise.

Expand It!

Show children examples or photos of the foods before or after the exercise. Use the proteins that are served for breakfast or lunch that day.

I Am Nutty!

Nuts are a good source of protein. Teach children about different types of nuts, what they look like, and how they are grown.

How to Do It

Note: *If you have children in your class who are allergic to nuts, make a point of telling the children that many people cannot eat nuts and get their healthy proteins in other yummy ways.*

1. Gather photos of different types of nuts to show to the children.
2. Show the children a picture of a peanut. Say the following and do the action to show the children what to do: "I am a peanut, I grow on a plant, and I am nutty!" Do a silly little "nutty" dance, bending over to touch the ground. Invite the children to pretend to be a peanut with you.
3. Have each child pick the kind of nut she would like to pretend to be:
    Peanut*(grows on a plant, then falls over toward the ground)
    Walnut (tree)
    Chestnut (tree)
    Cashew (tree)
    Brazil nut (tree)
    Almond (tree)
    Pistachio (tree)
    Pecan (tree)
    Hazelnut (shrub)
    Macadamia (tree)
    (Any nut that is available in your area)
    *Peanuts are not technically nuts; they are legumes. For our purposes, they will work for this activity.
4. As each child chooses a nut, show the children a photo of that nut. Encourage the children to move in the way they think a particular nut might move.

Pasta Wiggle

Good nutrition gives us energy, and the shapes are fun to make!

How to Do It

1. Ask the children to form a big circle. Ask them to raise their hands if they have ever eaten pasta, such as spaghetti. Tell them that pasta, especially whole-wheat pasta, is good for them.

2. Ask them if they know that pasta comes in lots of shapes. Let them describe some of the shapes that pasta can be found in. If possible, have some examples of uncooked pasta in a variety of shapes for the children to examine. Tell them that pasta changes as it cooks; it becomes softer.

3. Begin the exercise by asking the children to stand and make a stiff shape like an uncooked piece of spaghetti:

   Show me how straight and stiff spaghetti looks (stand stiffly like uncooked pasta) *before it is cooked!*

   Move around like you are uncooked! (Move around, walking stiffly)

   Now we drop the pasta into boiling water.

   Let's jump in! (Pretend to jump into hot water)

   As we soften, we make a wiggly shape. (Slowly form a wiggly shape)

   Now the pasta is fully cooked!

   Let's all do a wiggly dance! (Dance around like wiggly, squiggly cooked pasta!)

   Move around the room like a squiggly piece of cooked spaghetti! (Move around the room)

   Now come back to the circle. (Make a circle.)

Expand It!

- Repeat the exercise using different pasta shapes: ziti (tube), bowtie, short, long, lasagna (wide), wagon wheel, and so on. Go around the circle, and encourage the children to show you different shapes of pasta with their bodies.
- If your center allows, have some delicious whole-wheat pasta for lunch.

  Note: *Before serving food, be sure that the children do not have dietary restrictions.*

Whole grains, which still have their outer covering (the bran) and germ (high in nutrients), are a good source of fiber, vitamins, and minerals.

Brown Bread Better

Have fun with a tongue twister as you teach the children that brown grains are healthier for your body than processed (white) grains.

How to Do It

1. Explain to the children that grains such as wheat naturally grow brown. When grain is made white, most of the "best for your body" energy parts are stripped away. Brown grains give you energy.
2. Teach the children the following tongue twister: "Brown bread better." Challenge them to say it three times fast!
3. Stand up and shimmy and shake while chanting this tongue twister. After repeating it several times, say, "Freeze!" so this becomes a freeze dance. Start again.
4. Try repeating the chant with pasta, rice, and cereal: "Brown pasta better," "brown rice better," and "brown cereal better."

Making Healthy Stars

Make star shapes and star sandwiches, and let the children show what it means to be a star.

How to Do It

1. Before beginning, make sure to place some items around the room that are star shaped.
2. Ask the children what a star looks like. Can they point to anything in the room that is star shaped?
3. Can they make their bodies look like stars? Ask them to lie down on the floor and make stars (like snow angels)!
4. Tell them that healthy sandwiches can come in star shapes, too. Ask the children what they might put in their sandwiches. Let them suggest some ingredients, such as cheese or peanut butter and jelly, as they continue to make stars with their bodies.
5. Ask them to sit up and pretend to make their sandwiches, putting the ingredients on a slice of bread and then putting another slice of bread on top.
6. Tell them to pretend to use a cookie cutter to cut their sandwiches into star shapes.
7. Say, "Show me your sandwich!" and let the children pretend to show you their favorite sandwiches.

Expand It!

Make real star-shaped sandwiches for snack or lunch. Listen to "Twinkle, Twinkle Little Star" as you eat.

Sandwich Roll-Up

Encouraging healthy choices in kids' sandwiches as they learn and develop their core strength, flexibility of the spine, and coordination.

How to Do It

1. Ask the children to sit in a circle. Tap your knees to establish a rhythm, and encourage the children to join you.
2. Recite the following chant:
   Let's make a sandwich (Tap knees to the beat)
   And eat—it—up (Stretch out legs on *up*)
   Lay the bread flat (Slowly roll down onto back, bend knees)
   And ro-l-l-l it up! (Slowly sit up)
   Repeat several times.
3. After doing this exercise for some weeks, the children may be able to roll up without holding onto their legs. Any sort of rolling-up motion is fine and still gives the benefits of the exercise.

Expand It!

Ask children what kinds of things would be good and healthy in their sandwiches. Replace *Lay the bread flat* with *Put in some* (ingredient).

Pizza Pie in the Sky

Many children love pizza. Teach children that pizza can contain healthy ingredients and be yummy, too!

How to Do It

1. Ask the children to stand in a circle and pretend to hold a cup in their hands. Tell them that they are going to pretend to mix pizza dough and make pizzas.
2. Tell them that, first, they have to mix together water and flour. Let them pretend to pour the water and then flour from their cups into the center of the circle.
3. To mix the "dough" that the class has made, have all of the children hold hands and run around in a circle.
4. Encourage the children to pretend to throw the dough up in the air by raising their arms high, and then pretend to catch it a number of times.
5. Have them jump up and down to flatten the dough to make it round.
6. Next, have the children pretend to spread tomato sauce all around the center of the circle.
7. Let them choose some healthy toppings to add, such as mozzarella cheese, peppers, mushrooms, artichoke hearts, grilled chicken, feta cheese, sun-dried tomatoes, pineapple, ham, pesto, garlic, olives, onions, spinach, or tomatoes. Encourage them to act out sprinkling the cheese or spreading out the peppers and other toppings, moving into and out of the circle. Do this for each topping.
8. Pretend to carefully pick up the large pie and place it in an extra-large oven. Count to 10 or higher to "bake" the pizza, and then—ding!—take the pizza out of the oven. Count to 10 or higher to let it cool.
9. Let the children pretend to cut the pizza into slices to share.

Expand It!

Make an actual pizza for the children to enjoy. They can choose from among a selection of healthy toppings, and then you can show them how to divide a pizza into pieces, reinforcing the concepts of part and whole.

Water Break

Teach the children about the importance of drinking water throughout the day, especially before, during, and after exercise.

How to Do It

1. Ask the children to stand with enough room around them so they can move comfortably without running into each other.
2. Tell them that drinking enough water is very important, especially when they are running around and active. Tell them that, during this activity, they will pretend to have water breaks by running to a certain spot in the room. Indicate a place, and have them practice going there and returning to their spots when you say, "Water break!"
3. Ask the children to do a series of brief cardio exercises:

   Run in a circle

   Water break!

   Jump up and down

   Water break!

   Hop on one foot

   Water break!

   Kicks

   Water break!
4. Take the children for a well-deserved, real water break.

The Milk March

Teach the children about different healthy milk choices.

How to Do It

1. Read a book about how milk is produced for market, such as *Milk: From Cow to Carton* by Aliki. Talk with the children about how a cow gives milk and that milk is processed for people to drink.
2. Ask the children to stand and join hands to make an assembly line for processing milk.
3. Ask them to move their joined hands up and down to make the milk go around in the large vats of the milk machines.
4. Ask them to drop hands and then rub their hands together as if warming up the milk to be heated up in a vat and then back to the tubes.
5. Join hands again and march in a circle. Then break the circle at one point, and march in a line around the room, pretending to shop for different kinds of milk: low-fat, skim, and soymilk.

Expand It!

Have milk or soymilk at snack time. Let the children practice pouring the milk into cups.

To build strong bones and teeth, the U.S. Department of Agriculture (website: www.ChooseMyPlate.gov) recommends low-fat (1%) or nonfat (skim) milk and calcium-enriched soymilk as healthy sources of calcium, potassium, phosphorus, and vitamin D. Chocolate milk contains empty calories from sugar. Plain milk is a healthier alternative.

Drink, Droop, Drop!

Teach children about the effects of sugary drinks on the body.

How to Do It

1. Ask the children if they know of any sugary drinks such as sodas, vitamin water, or fruit-flavored drinks. (Note: You may have to explain to the children that drinking some 100 percent juice is okay.) Listen to their responses. Tell them that too much sugar is not good for them. Sugar gives us a short burst of energy, but that does not last long, and sugar does not give us the vitamins and other nutrients we need.

2. Ask the children to stand in a circle. Ask them to pretend to drink a sugary drink. (If the drink has bubbles, bounce up and down.)

3. Ask them to run in place as you count to five. Tell them that you are running out of energy!

4. Gradually slow down, drooping more and more, and drop to the ground, lying flat on the floor. Say, "Oh, no! I'm so tired! I don't have any more energy!"

5. Repeat, pretending to drink other sugary drinks. Continue as long as the children are interested.

The American Association of Pediatrics recommends that children ages one through six years consume no more than 4 to 6 ounces of 100 percent fruit juice per day. Whole fruit is a better alternative, as it offers fiber as well as nutrients.

Mash It Up! Mix It Up! That's a Smoothie!

Children can have fun pretending to make fruit smoothies and then can make the real thing or have some premade smoothies to try.

How to Do It

1. Ask the children if they have ever tried a fruit smoothie. If they do not know what a smoothie is, explain that it is a mixture of mashed-up fruit, fruit juice, and yogurt. It is sweet and delicious to drink!

2. Tell them they are going to pretend to make a smoothie. Ask them to imagine that they are holding a handful of their favorite fruit. They may choose bananas, strawberries, blueberries, or other varieties. Ask the children what fruits they are holding—ask them about the colors of their fruit and how their fruits taste. Ask them how many pieces of fruit they have, and count the imaginary pieces with them.

3. Tell them they need to squeeze and mash their fruit to make a smoothie. Encourage them to pretend to mash the fruit in their hands and then add it to an imaginary cup.

4. Now tell them that they need to add some juice. Ask them what kind of juice they would like to add: perhaps orange, grape, or apple. Tell them, "Let's squeeze up some juice! Squeeze hard to get all the juice out!" Do the Juicy Squeeze It Up Dance, encouraging the children to stomp, squeeze, and wiggle.

5. Ask them if they would like to add a little yogurt to their smoothies, to make them creamy. Some children may choose to add yogurt; others may not. Either choice is fine and will make a delicious smoothie. Pretend to add yogurt, counting how many spoonfuls: one, two, three, four, five!

6. Say, "Now we need to mix up our smoothies!" Do a Mix-It-Up Dance, wiggling and spinning around.

Expand It!

If possible, let the children select and add the ingredients to make real smoothies with a variety of fresh fruit, 100 percent fruit juice, and low-fat or nonfat yogurt. Mix the smoothies in a blender for them, and let them taste their creations.

The Right Time for Dessert

Teach the children that a sweet treat is okay once in a while, but only after eating healthy foods.

How to Do It

1. Ask the children to sit with you in a circle. Pretend to have a tummy ache. Say, "Oh! I ate cake and cookies and ice cream for breakfast! Now my tummy hurts! I don't feel good!" Ask the children, "Did I make a good choice for breakfast?" Let them tell you that you did not make a good choice, and ask them to tell you some better choices. If necessary, guide them toward healthy choices such as fresh fruit, whole-grain cereal or toast, low-fat or nonfat yogurt, and milk.

2. Ask them, "When is the right time for dessert?" Guide them through a discussion by offering different times:
   - Right after I brush my teeth (pretend to brush): Is that a good time for dessert? No!
   - Lunchtime (pretend to eat): Is that a good time for dessert? No! What about after I eat a healthy lunch of soup and sandwich and fruit? Yes! That would be the right time.
   - Snack: Is that a good time for dessert? No!
   - Dinner: Is that the right time for dessert? No! What about after I eat a healthy dinner of grilled chicken, salad, and brown rice? Yes! That would be the right time.
   - I already had one dessert today (pretend to lick an ice cream cone): Could I have another? No! One sweet treat is enough!
   - Bedtime (pretend to sleep): Is that the right time for dessert? No!

3. Let the children offer times in the day, and then discuss with them whether or not those times would be right for dessert.

Make Transitions Fun

Children often struggle with transitions from one activity to another. When the transition involves waiting, they can have an even harder time. Turn any transition time into useful time with actions. Not only will you be incorporating movement into their day, but you also will be keeping them occupied and entertained.

Moving and Grooving

- Swing those arms—Children use big arm swings as they walk or march
- Clapping those hands—Clap hands to the beat of the walk or march
- Punch the clouds—Lift arms overhead, alternating punching arms in the air, while walking or marching
- Hold up those arms—Walk or march with arms up in air overhead, two arms moving side to side together
- Happy head walk—Walk or march with arms at the sides and moving the upper body side to side.
- Tap head and shoulders—Tap head and then tap shoulders while walking or marching
- Airplane arms—Hold arms out to the sides and then bring them back in to the body in rhythm with walking or marching
- Big-knee march—March while lifting knees high
- Big-knee march with arms—Use both hands to push each knee down as you do the big knee march
- Math enrichment—Add counting to any of the Moving and Grooving activities
- Literacy enrichment—Add letters to any of the Moving and Grooving activities

Chanting and Moving

Add a chant as you move (to the tune of "The Farmer in the Dell"):
I walk (or march or skip) *myself around,*
I walk myself around.
I walk and walk and walk some more,
I walk myself around.

Galloping and Skipping

Galloping and skipping take a little practice. Younger children will approximate the movements; older children will be able to gallop and skip.

- Gallop like a horse—Gallop with one foot leading to front
- Side gallop—Gallop with body turned sideways
- Airplane arms gallop—Gallop and keep arms open in a straight line
- Arms out and in gallop—Gallop while stretching arms out, then bringing them back in to the body
- Skipping and swinging—Skip with big arm actions
- Push and skip—Skip while pushing arms forward, alternating arms
- Happy head skip—Skip while using big arms and moving the upper body and head side to side

Move for Motor Skills

Use movement to help children focus, ready to learn with both mind and body. Encouraging children to touch parts of their faces and bodies wakes up the proprioceptive nervous system and stimulates the focus of different body parts and senses.

Focusing and Calming

Legs and Arms

Core and Cardiovascular

Body Patterns and Spatial Awareness

Calming and Ending

Let's Get Ready to Learn

Use this chant as a way to capture the children's attention and get them focused at the start of the day.

How to Do It

Invite the children to gather with you as you say this chant:

I am ready to learn now,

And I see you are, too.

Let's put on our listening ears. (touch ears)

Ding, ding, ding, ding, ding.

Let's put on our watching eyes. (touch eyelids)

Ding, ding, ding, ding, ding.

Let's put on a funny nose, boop! (touch nose)

And our mouth. (tap open mouth, making "wawawa" sound)

Let's put on our big feet! (bend knees and tap feet loudly on floor)

Let's put on our tiny feet! (tap feet quietly on floor)

Let's put on our flying arms. (hold out arms and flap gently)

And our flying fingers. (flutter fingers with arms outstretched)

I am ready to learn now,

And I see you are, too!

Good Morning, Toes

A great way to focus the children and get them ready for the day.

How to Do It

1. Ask children to sit in a circle and stretch their legs out in front of them.
2. Show the children how to point their toes. Tell them that when their toes are pointed, their feet are "sleeping."
3. Show them how to flex their feet. Tell them that when their feet are flexed, they are "awake."
4. Teach the children the following chant:
   Good morning, little toes! (Speak loudly, flex feet)
   Good night, little toes. (Whisper, point toes)
   Good morning, little toes! (Flex)
   Good night, little toes. (Point)
   Oh, no! I see our toes
   have fallen back to sleep. (Toes remain pointed)
   Let's tickle them
   to wake them up! (Reach to touch toes, gently tickle)
5. Flex your feet and say, "Ah! Mine woke up! Let me see yours!" Encourage the children to flex their feet.

Working with Children Who Have Limited Movement
Remember: For children who have a limited range of movement, highlight the positive aspects of what they can do. Encourage them to participate as much as they are able, and show appreciation for their efforts.

Five-Finger Focus

Simple, easy-to-remember rules for the class can calm and focus the children, and help develop fine-motor skills.

How to Do It

1. Use these five rules or create your own. Ask the children to sit in a circle or group.
2. Hold up a fist and ask the children to tell you how many fingers you have. Uncurl each finger as you count together: one, two, three, four, five.
3. Tell the children there are five rules for the class. Teach them the following list:
    - Hold up your thumb: One—I am here and ready for the day.
    - Add the index finger: Two—When the teacher talks, I listen quietly.
    - Add the middle finger: Three—I raise a silent hand when I have a question.
    - Add the ring finger: Four—I always put away my things.
    - Add the pinky: Five—I am kind to myself and others.
4. Ask the children to go through the list with you again, using their fingers as they count.
5. Reward the children for their quiet attention by encouraging them to stand up and wiggle their fingers, hands, arms, and whole bodies.

Expand It!

Have the children help you develop five good rules for a classroom, or use this technique to create five rules for a certain activity or field trip.

Hello Stretching

Use this simple stretch to greet the children and help them focus.

How to Do It

1. Ask the children sit in a circle with a little space between them so they can move.
2. Ask them to stretch out their legs in a V shape in front of them. They should sit so that their legs are comfortably wide apart.
3. Ask them to sit up tall and stretch their arms up, up, up in the air.
4. Encourage the children to stretch their upper bodies over to one leg, while staying in the V shape.
5. Encourage them to stretch an arm over their heads and wave hello to the child next to them.
6. Encourage the children to stretch their upper bodies over the other leg, while staying in the V shape.
7. Stretch the other arm overhead and wave hello to the child next to them on the other side.
8. Come back to the middle with arms stretching up, up, up again. Wave and say hello to the whole class!

Stretching Safety Tips
- Warm up before stretching: fast walk, run, or gallop in place.
- Only stretch as far as is comfortable. Do not force or push the muscles. Tell the children to stop if it hurts.
- Stretch slowly.
- Do not bounce into the stretch.
- Breathe while stretching; model the breathing and tell the children to breathe in and out.
- Stretch the whole body, not just the parts that will be used in a particular exercise.

Everybody Line Up!

Line-up time can be a physical activity, too.

How to Do It

1. When you call the children to line up, give them an action to use to get to the line. For example, ask them to do one of the following:
   - Jump
   - Gallop
   - Hop
   - Sway side to side while walking
   - Skip
   - Fly
   - Float like a balloon

2. Alternatively, call out a characteristic that can identify some, but not all, of the children. For example:
   - Anyone wearing blue today, float like a balloon to the line.
   - Anyone wearing sneakers today, fly to the line.
   - Anyone who likes to eat grapes, skip to the line.
   - Anyone who likes to eat salad like a bunny, hop to the line.

3. Surprise the children by changing your instruction each time you use this activity.

Be a Statue

Use this activity to help children develop balance and to calm them after more active learning and play.

How to Do It

1. Ask the children to stand well spaced in the room. Tell the children they will be statues, freezing in place.
2. Begin by asking the children to stand up tall. Ask them to pick a simple, easy pose that they can hold for a minute or two. Tell them to freeze.
3. Tell them to unfreeze and give themselves a hug. And freeze!
4. Tell them to unfreeze and hug their arms over their heads. And freeze!
5. Tell them to unfreeze, clap their hands over their heads, and hold them there. And freeze!
6. Tell them to unfreeze and keep their statue hands glued together, but put their hands on their tummies. And freeze!
7. Tell them to unfreeze, relax, and take a deep breath in and out.
8. Ask them to be statues again and to stand with their legs crossed. And freeze!
9. Tell them to unfreeze and try to stand with their legs crossed and their hands clapped above their heads. And freeze!
10. Tell them to unfreeze, relax, and take a deep breath in and out. Now wiggle!

Elephants

Help the children improve balance, eye-hand coordination, and attention.

How to Do It

1. Ask the children to stand well-spaced in the middle of the room. Tell them they will be elephants, and use one of their arms as a long elephant trunk.
2. Ask them to hold up an arm and move slowly around like elephants.
3. Ask them to draw some pictures in the air with their elephant trunks. Encourage them to draw the letter *O*. Draw a big circle in the air with one arm.
4. Next, draw the letter *M*. Gently move one arm and focus on going up, down, up, down.
5. Draw the letter *X*. Do it with curves so it is like a figure eight in the air.
6. Change arms and draw with the other arm.
7. Continue in this manner, drawing letters or numbers in the air.

Expand It!

Focus on drawing letters or numbers that your class is learning.

Slo-Mo Moving

Wake up the brain with cross-body patterning.

How to Do It

1. Ask the children if they have heard of *slow motion*. Let one or two children tell you what slow motion is. If no one knows, tell the children that slow motion is walking or moving in place very, very slowly. Demonstrate for them.
2. Tell them that they will pretend they are moving around on the moon in slow motion, as if they are running through pudding! On the moon, everything moves really slowly. Encourage them to walk slowly in place.
3. Encourage them to run slowly in place. Tell them to move as if they are running but do it in slow motion.
4. Encourage them to pretend they want to run side to side, but they are stuck in place. Tell them to make their arms and legs move slowly to one side and then to the other side.
5. Ask them to try marching in slow motion.

Thumbs Up!

Help the children focus and pay attention, improve vision skills, and improve eye-hand coordination.

How to Do It

1. Ask the children to sit or stand, facing you.
2. Hold up your thumbs and ask the children to watch you and follow your thumbs with their watching eyes.
3. Put your fists together, thumbs up, and move your thumbs up and down, side to side, and in a circle in one direction and then the other.
4. Ask the children to hold up their own two thumbs in front of their faces. Ask them to follow the movement of their thumbs with their watching eyes.
5. Ask them to put their fists together, thumbs up, and move up and down, side to side, and in a circle in one direction and then the other.
6. Tell them to take their thumbs for a trip to their ears. Tell them to find their ears with their fingers, one hand on each ear. Encourage them to rub their ears and do a little dance with their fingers on their ears.
7. Tell them to give themselves a thumbs-up for using seeing eyes and listening ears, then to take a deep breath in and out and shake out their arms.

Tapping Crossed and Open

Encourage concentration as you focus on a rhythmic, cross-bodied fine motor skill.

How to Do It

1. Do not worry about the perfect execution of this task. It is a means to focus and allow the brain to work through a new pattern and process.
2. Ask the children to sit in a circle. Encourage them to tap their knees. Start by tapping the right hand on the right knee and the left hand on the left knee at the same time. Repeat until the class is in sync.
3. Encourage them to cross their arms so that the right hand taps the left knee and the left hand taps the right knee. Keep arms crossed and continue tapping until the class is in sync.
4. Challenge them to try tapping their knees with arms crossing and opening, crossing and opening. Repeat until the class is in sync.

Cat Back

Engage the core muscles and stretch the spine in a fun way.

How to Do It

1. Ask the children to sit on the floor. Ask them to get into a position like a cat, on their hands and knees.
2. Ask them to show how a cat stretches its back. Encourage them to touch their chins to chests and pull their tummies up toward their spines.
3. Ask them to reverse the stretch and look up, arching in the opposite direction, tummies toward the floor, and looking up.
4. Reverse the stretch again, tucking chins to chests and pulling tummies toward spines.
5. Encourage them to show how a happy kitty looks. Arch the back, stick out the tail, and smile. Then reverse, tucking chins to chests and pulling tummies toward spines.
6. Continue in this manner, letting the children try stretching and arching like cats.
7. Encourage the children to wiggle their tails from side to side, then curl up on the floor and take a cat nap.

Down Dog

Help the children learn how to engage the core muscles while stretching the backs of the legs.

How to Do It

1. Ask the children to sit in a circle. Tell them they will pretend to be puppies, stretching after a nap.
2. Ask them get on their hands and knees. When they get into the position, ask them to spread their palms like puppy paws on the floor, put their feet on the floor, and lift their hips to the sky.
3. Encourage them to stick out their tongues and pant like puppies, wiggle their tails from side to side, and bark as if they were puppies.
4. Encourage them to take four doggie steps forward, to bark like puppies, and to wag their happy puppy tails.
5. Encourage them to take four doggie steps backward, then walk around the room like puppies.

Expand It!

Challenge the children to balance on three legs (one hand and two feet or two hands and one foot), without falling over. Repeat on the other side.

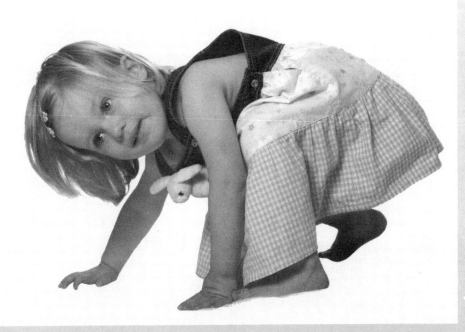

V-Sit Stretch

Stretch the leg muscles and wake up the body.

How to Do It

1. Ask the children to sit in a big circle. Ask them to sit with their legs in a V out to the sides to stretch inner thigh muscles.
2. Ask them to stretch their arms out to the sides, like airplanes, then tip to the left to stretch the sides of the waist.
3. Ask them to come back to center, bringing their bodies upright. Breathe in and out.
4. Tip to the other side to stretch the sides of the waist, then come back to center. Breathe in and out.
5. Encourage them to put their hands on the floor between their legs, then walk their fingers toward the center of the circle.
6. Next, walk their fingers back and sit up straight. Breathe in and out.

Yawning and Stretching

Yawning brings oxygen to the brain and then to the body.

How to Do It

1. Ask the children to sit in a circle. Ask the children to show you what a yawn looks like.
2. Encourage them to put their hands on their cheeks and rub. Then ask them to open their mouths wide and yawn.
3. Encourage them to rub their cheeks again and to open their mouths wide and yawn, a little bigger this time.
4. Try one more time, this time yawning as big as they can.
5. Encourage them to stretch their arms up to the sky, then take a big breath in and breathe out.
6. Ask them to stand up and stretch their arms up to the sky, feeling as tall as a tree from hands to feet. Take a deep breath in and out.
7. Ask them to raise their arms up, then lower their arms down. Repeat. Take a deep breath in and out. Raise and lower their arms again.

Open and Close Stretch

Help the children learn how to stretch their legs and back muscles in a seated position.

How to Do It

1. Ask the children to sit well spaced in a circle. Encourage them to sit up tall with legs extended to the center of the room, stretching their knees and showing their heels.
2. Ask them to reach their fingertips to the center of the room, stretching their arms out in the front and reaching over their toes.
3. Encourage them to slowly open their arms and legs to make a V, then close their arms and legs again.
4. Ask them to slowly bend and reach for their toes again, then sit up tall.
5. Repeat in this manner several times.

Long Legs and Short Legs

Sharpen children's listening skills and reaction time, as well as attention to detail.

How to Do It

1. Ask the children to sit in a circle.
2. Hug your knees to your chest with your arms, and keep your feet on the floor as you sit in a little ball. Encourage the children to do the same.
3. Say, "Let's make our legs very long." Stretch your legs out in front of you.
4. Say, "Let's make our legs very short." Pull your legs in toward your chest.
5. Repeat, increasing the length of the word *long* and pausing before saying, "Short!"
6. Make a game of it by shortening and lengthening the pauses between *long* and *short,* so the children have to listen attentively to know when to stretch their legs or bring their knees to their chests.
7. Switch to alternating legs, lengthening one leg while keeping the other leg hugged to the chest.
8. Switch legs as fast as the children can, hugging one leg at a time.

Expand It!

Do the same exercise while sitting, whenever the children need a short break. Change the instructions to *stand up* and *sit down*.

I Was a Baby, and Now I'm Big!

Promote a healthy body image and the realization for children that they have already achieved physical abilities simply by growing from baby to child.

How to Do It

1. Ask the children to lie down on the floor on their backs. Invite them to pretend that they are little-bitty new babies. Encourage them to roll into little balls on their backs and pretend that they are wrapped up in blankets, safe and warm. Encourage them to make faces like they imagine a baby would make and to make sounds like a baby would make.

2. Encourage them to pretend that they are older babies: put their feet in the air, touch their feet with their hands, and roll side to side.

3. Next, they can pretend that they are learning to roll over onto their tummies. Encourage them to roll over and back several times.

4. Say, "Look, now you are stronger and can sit up!" Encourage them to practice lying down and then sitting up.

5. Encourage them to scoot around on their bottoms. Then, encourage them to get ready to crawl: "Go up on your hands and knees! Rock back and forth a little."

6. Ask them to pretend that they can crawl, slowly at first and then faster. Crawl to one side of the room and then all around the room.

7. Tell them that after babies learn to crawl, they can hold themselves erect while on their knees. "Up and down, onto your knees, and then back down to the floor!" Encourage them to try walking around on their knees.

8. They are finally ready to try walking. Tell them, "Babies stand up by holding onto something or someone. Let's go to a chair or table and hold on. Stand up slowly." Let them try walking slowly, then gradually walking faster and faster until they are running around the room in a big circle.

9. Tell them that they are now big kids, and big kids deserve a rest after all that exercise! Take a water break!

Use Your Muscles

Teach the children where their muscles are and how using them makes them strong.

How to Do It

1. Invite the children to sit in a well-spaced circle. Tell them they will use their muscles, and show them how to find the muscles on their arms and legs.
Tell them that their muscles move their body parts. Moving muscles helps make the muscles strong.
2. Ask them to bend their arms and to feel the muscles as they move. Do this several times.
3. Ask them to lift up one leg, then the other, and to feel their muscles working. Now ask them to lift both legs up and to hold them up—that takes a lot of work!
4. Encourage them to shake out their arms and legs.

Pass the "Foot" Ball

Help children develop coordination and core and leg strength.

How to Do It

1. You will need a medium-sized ball for this activity. It will work best if the ball is a little squishy.
2. Ask the children to sit in a circle. Show the children how to lift up their legs and to hold the ball between their feet. Let them each practice holding the ball with their feet.
3. Once they have the hang of the activity, encourage them to pass the ball around the circle, using only their feet.
4. Go around the circle until each child has had a turn.

Walk This Way

Make transitions from place to place more fun by varying your pace.

How to Do It

1. Ask the children to line up behind you. Walk in a straight line, establishing a regular pace, for 30 seconds.
2. Change the pace of your steps, telling the children what you will do. Choose several to try from the following list:
   - walk very slowly
   - walk very fast
   - walk with arms and legs staying rigid and straight
   - walk in a step-jump pattern
   - walk and turn at the same time
   - walk with hands and feet (on all fours)
   - walk low to the ground (duck walk)
   - walk with the same arm as the leg swinging forward
   - walk with giant steps
   - walk with tiny steps
   - walk on your tiptoes

Expand It!

Ask the line leader for the day to choose how the class will walk from place to place.

Walk like an Animal

Try this variation of the game Charades.

How to Do It

1. Ask the children to sit in a circle. Have each child take a turn walking like her favorite animal. Encourage the other children to guess the animal.
2. If the children have trouble thinking of the ways animals move, whisper suggestions from the following list:
   - elephant: bend over, swinging one arm like a trunk
   - tiger or lion: crawl on all fours, slowly and carefully
   - alligator: lie on tummy and push with arms and legs, opening mouth wide
   - snake or eel: lie on tummy with arms at sides and wiggle to move around
   - monkey: pretend to swing from tree branches
   - dog: crawl on all fours and wag "tail"
   - turtle: pretend to swim using arms and legs to propel body, come up for air
   - squirrel or raccoon: crawl on all fours, stopping to sit on haunches and pretend to eat with hands
   - deer or antelope: leap around the room

Judy Willis, in her book *How Your Child Learns Best: Brain-Friendly Strategies You Can Use to Ignite Your Child's Learning and Increase School Success*, says that the dopamine—the chemical the brain produces in response to something pleasurable—released when children are actively engaged in an activity increases their capacity to control attention and store long-term memories.

If You're Happy and You Know It

Reinforce rhythm and pattern learning with the endless variations of this familiar song.

How to Do It

1. Ask the children to stand in a big circle. Teach the children the following song:
   If you're happy and you know it, clap your hands!
   If you're happy and you know it, clap your hands!
   If you're happy and you know it,
   and you'd really like to show it,
   If you're happy and you know it, clap your hands!

2. Continue singing, adding movements to change each verse:
   - clap hands
   - stomp feet
   - nod head
   - wave arms
   - wiggle behind
   - turn around
   - hop on one foot

Expand It!

Encourage volunteers to choose an action and lead the class in the song.

Picking Up Pawpaws

Reinforce coordination, core strength, rhythm, and listening skills.

How to Do It

1. Teach the children the following song:
   Where, oh where is dear little Nellie?
   Where, oh where is dear little Nellie?
   Where, oh where is dear little Nellie?
   Way down yonder in the pawpaw patch!
   Pickin' up pawpaws, put 'em in your pocket.
   Pickin' up pawpaws, put 'em in your pocket.
   Pickin' up pawpaws, put 'em in your pocket.
   Way down yonder in the pawpaw patch!
   Come on, children, let's go find her!
   Come on, children, let's go find her!
   Come on, children, let's go find her!
   Way down yonder in the pawpaw patch!

2. Sing the song again, this time inserting a child's name.
   Where, oh where is dear little (name)? (Bring hand to forehead, search around)
   Where, oh where is dear little (name)? (search)
   Where, oh where is dear little (name)? (search)
   Way down yonder in the pawpaw patch! (Point and run to the side of the room)
   Pickin' up pawpaws, put 'em in her pocket. (Bend down and pick up, put in pocket)
   Pickin' up pawpaws, put 'em in her pocket. (Bend down and pick up, put in pocket.)
   Pickin' up pawpaws, put 'em in her pocket. Bend down and pick up, put in pocket.)
   Way down yonder in the pawpaw patch! (Run back to the circle.)
   Come on, children, let's go find her! (Hold hands in a circle.)
   Come on, children, let's go find her! (Skip around in a circle.)
   Come on, children, let's go find her! (Skip around in a circle.)
   Way down yonder in the pawpaw patch! (Clap your hands and jump three times)

3. Continue as long as the children are interested, inserting a different name each time.

Tap, Tap, Move!

This activity is a variation of the game Duck, Duck, Goose! that teaches gross motor skills and encourages social skills.

How to Do It

1. Ask the children to sit in a circle. Choose a volunteer to be a tapper, or demonstrate yourself for the first turn.
2. The tapper walks around the circle, tapping each child on the shoulder and saying, "Tap, tap, tap," as he goes.
3. The tapper stops at a child and says, "Move!" The child tapped with *move* gets up and imitates the action that the tapper makes. For example, the tapper may turn around three times or hop on one foot or duck-walk around the circle. The sillier the action, the better!
4. The tapper then sits down in the circle, and the new tapper continues the game.

Machine Word Game

Promote cooperation as you build the children's vocabulary.

How to Do It

1. Ask the children to stand in a circle. Tell them that they will each be parts in a big machine. Ask them what their machine might make: toy trucks? bicycles? blocks? jump ropes?

2. Tell the children that their machine will operate by their body movements. Call out a body part and show them a movement to do when they hear that body part name. Start with three movements and then add movements as the children become comfortable with the activity.
   - Hands: clap
   - Fingers: make fist and open
   - Legs: bend and straighten
   - Heads: look to one side, then the other
   - Arms: reach up, then down
   - Hips: bend to one side, then the other

3. Ask the children to imitate your movements as you call out the body parts. Do this several times until the children have the hang of it.

4. Add silly sounds to each movement, such as the following:
   - Hands: clapping noise
   - Fingers: children say, "Beep!"
   - Legs: children say, "Boing!"
   - Heads: children say, "Boop! Boop!"
   - Arms: children say, "Whee! Whee!"
   - Hips: children say, "Swish! Swish!"

   Practice the movements and sounds together several times.

5. Now put it all together. Do the machine movements and sounds several times. The children may stand and face the center of the circle, they may turn and face the back of the child in front of them, or they may do the actions in pairs.

Basketball Jumps

Use leg and arm strength to throw an imaginary basketball into an imaginary hoop.

How to Do It

1. Ask the children to line up on one side of the room. Tell them to imagine there is a basketball hoop on the wall of the opposite side of the room.
2. Ask them to pretend they are holding a ball and shooting it into the basket. Encourage them to jump high as they shoot, pretending that someone is lifting them up in the air from the bottom of their spines.
3. Encourage them to circle back to the end of the line and wait for another turn.

Galloping

Galloping is the bridge between running and skipping. Encourage the children to use the rhythm of galloping as they develop the skills for skipping.

How to Do It

1. Ask the children to stand in a circle. Tell them that they will gallop like horses. Show them how to gallop, and let them try the movement.
2. Ask them to return to the circle and place their hands on their hips. Ask them to turn to the right. (Show younger children which way to turn so that all of the children are facing front to back.)
3. Encourage them to gallop around the circle. You may choose to clap to a beat or play some music for them to gallop to.
4. Ask them to turn around and gallop the other direction.
5. Ask them to face toward the center of the circle and gallop sideways, first one direction and then the other.
6. Continue in this manner as long as the children are having fun.

Expand It!

During transitions, gallop from place to place instead of walking.

Good Health Begins Early

Experts agree—A healthy lifestyle begins when children are young. Model healthy eating habits, and incorporate physical activity throughout the day.

Jumping Over the River

Learning how to leap takes time and practice. Two- and three-year olds usually do not get very far off the ground, but older children will be able to take to the air.

How to Do It

1. Ask the children to stand in a line in one corner of the room. Tell them there is a wide imaginary river in the middle of the room, and they must leap across it.
2. Show them how to run and leap to the other corner. Tell them, "Leap over the river so you don't get wet!"
3. Practice this exercise together as a group, with the children leaping all at once. Then, let the children take turns leaping over the river.

Rock 'n' Roll Jumps

Encourage the children to channel their inner rock stars.

How to Do It

1. Ask the children to stand in a line against a wall. Ask them if they know what a rock-star jump is. Show them your best rock-star jump! (They will *love* seeing this!)
2. Ask the children to take turns showing you their best rock-star jumps. Let each child take a running start and make a big kicking jump in the air.
3. After their jumps, let them run to the other side of the room.
4. When everyone has had a turn, do it back the other way.

Expand It!

Consider playing some lively music to inspire their best jumps.

I Get a Kick Out of You

Help the children develop their sense of balance and gross motor skills as they try these kicks.

How to Do It: Donkey Kicks

1. Ask the children to stand spaced well apart in the room. Make sure no child is behind another.
2. Show them how to put their hands on the floor and kick up one leg and then the other, like a donkey. If they wish, they can say, "Hee-haw!" as they do it.

How to Do It: Hat Dance Kicks

1. Play some lively music, such as Mexican hat dance music. Ask the children to put their hands on their hips and bounce to the beat.
2. Add a twisting motion, twisting side to side.
3. Show the children how to move across the room in one of the following ways:
   - Step three times and kick (repeat)
   - Step, kick, step, kick (repeat)
   - Kick, kick (repeat)
4. First, try it as a group in a line formation. Next, ask the children to move across one by one or with a partner.

Kick Line!

Help the children develop balance, rhythm, and coordination.

How to Do It

1. Ask the children to stand in a line on one side of the room.
2. Encourage them to stand up straight and tall. Ask them to put their hands on their hips.
3. Ask them to kick one leg up and down several times. Encourage them to concentrate on keeping their balance as they kick.
4. Next, ask them to kick the other leg up and down several times.
5. Ask them to try kicking by alternating legs: one then the other.
6. Play some music, and let them try to kick to the beat.

Snakes in the Grass

Children will build upper body and core strength as they do this imaginative stretching exercise.

How to Do It

1. Ask the children to lie on the floor in a tight circle, heads facing you as you sit in the center. Tell the children they are going to pretend to be snakes, wriggling on their bellies in the grass. They will need space to move backward into a larger circle and then in again to the smaller circle.
2. Ask the children what sound a snake makes. Encourage the children to hiss like snakes.
3. Ask them to move backward, pushing with their arms as they move on their bellies like snakes.
4. Tell them to look up, lifting their upper bodies by pushing with their hands. Say, "Oh, I think I see a hawk!" Encourage the children to look around. "Better hide!" Encourage the children to lower their upper bodies and put their heads on the floor.
5. Ask them to raise their upper bodies again and move forward into a tight circle again. Then tell them, "Look up! I see an elephant! Don't want to get stepped on!" Encourage them to drop their heads to the floor.
6. Continue in this manner, asking the children to move backward and forward, lifting their upper bodies with their arms and then dropping to the floor again. Imagine that you see all sorts of animals, such as monkeys and lions. Ask the children to name an animal that the "snakes" see.

Have a Ball!

Develop core strength and directional learning.

How to Do It

1. Ask the children to sit cross-legged on the floor, with plenty of room around them so they will not bump into each other.
2. Ask them to rock their bodies side to side, pushing off the floor with their hands.
3. Ask them to hug their knees to their chests and rock forward and back without falling over. Ask them to rock side to side without falling over.
4. Ask them to reach into the air and rock side to side without falling over.
5. Ask them to rock in a circle, keeping their legs crossed and supporting themselves with their hands if they need to.

Expand It!

1. Ask the children to sit in a line on one side of the room. If the class size is large, ask the children to do this in groups of three.
2. Ask the children to lie down and log-roll to the other side of the room and back.
3. If they are comfortable doing forward rolls, they can try rolling across the room.

Starfish, Jellyfish

Encourage gross motor development, balance, and core strength with this "fishy" activity.

How to Do It

1. Ask the children to sit in a circle. Tell them that they will pretend to be starfish and jellyfish.
2. Ask them to hug their knees tightly to their chests and balance in this position. Now tell them to keep their knees tucked while wiggling their arms and legs around in front of themselves like jellyfish.
3. Ask them to keep wiggling arms and legs as they slowly melt their jelly bodies into the floor until they are lying on their backs.
4. To pretend to be starfish, ask them to sit up quickly, trying to balance while seated with their legs and arms held out straight from their bodies like starfish.
5. Next, have fun calling out *jellyfish* and *starfish*, challenging the children to switch back and forth as they imitate each animal.

Bendy Bodies Stretch

Use this activity whenever the children need to wake up their minds and bodies.

How to Do It

1. Ask the children to stand in a big circle.
2. Encourage them to imitate your movements as you stretch and breathe:
   - Stretch way up high, and reach hands up to the sky.
   - Take a big breath in and let it out. Breathe in and out.
   - Bend and touch toes.
   - Stand up tall, and reach hands to the sky.
   - Bend to one side, then bend to the other side.
   - Stretch arms out and step, feet far apart. Bring arms and legs back in.
   - Stretch way up high, and reach hands up to the sky.
   - Take a big breath in and let it out. Breathe in and out.
   - Bend and touch toes.
   - Stand up tall, and reach hands to the sky.

   Note: For children who have limited movement, encourage them to stretch and reach as much as they are able.

Balance like Me

Help children develop the core strength to balance in different positions.

How to Do It

1. Ask the children to stand in a big circle. Teach them the following chant:
   Balance and balance and balance like me!
   Balance and balance, what do you see?
   Balance and balance and balance like me!
   Balance and balance, I see a tree!
   Balance and balance and balance like me!
   Balance and balance, I see a statue!

2. Tell them that you will name different objects, and each time you will all freeze in a pose that is like that object; for example:
   Balance and balance and balance like me! (Bounce knees to the rhythm)
   Balance and balance, what do you see? (Freeze in a balance pose, object of choice).
   Balance and balance and balance like me! (Bounce your knees to the rhythm)
   Balance and balance, I see a tree! (Freeze in a tree pose)
   Balance and balance and balance like me! (Bounce your knees to the rhythm)
   Balance and balance, I see a statue! (Freeze like a statue)

Expand It!

Encourage volunteers to say the rhyme and choose a pose for the class to do.

Posture Caps

Encourage good posture and health through spinal alignment.

How to Do It

1. Ask the children to stand and touch their backs to feel the straight line of the spine in the center of their back. Tell them that it goes from the top of their back under the head all the way to the bottom of the back.

2. Ask them if they can feel the little bones in their spines. Do the bones feel hard or soft? Talk about how the hard bones hold us tall but also let us move around in many directions. Encourage the children to wiggle around as they move their spines.

3. Tell the children that the bones in their spines sit on top of each other like little caps.

   Ask them to stand up straight and tall and to pretend that they are putting caps on their heads. What color do they want their caps to be?

4. Ask the children to walk straight and tall to keep their caps on their heads.

5. Ask them to pretend to add some more caps on top of their heads. Ask, "How many caps do you think we can add and balance on our heads?" Encourage them to guess how many they could balance on their heads. Count the caps together as you pretend to put them on.

6. Walk around, balancing the imaginary caps as they walk straight and tall.

Walking the Line

Encourage balancing and eye-foot coordination while enhancing spatial awareness.

How to Do It

1. Tape a long, straight line on your floor, or use one that you already have. Alternatively, place one chair on one side of the room and another chair on the other side of the room and have children imagine a line that connects in between them.
2. Ask the children to stand against a wall on one side of the room.
3. Ask the children to take turns walking the length of the line, trying to keep their feet on the line like a tightrope walker. It is not imperative that the children stay exactly on the line; it is the effort that counts.
4. When all of the children have had a turn, ask them to come back in the other direction, walking like tightrope walkers down the line.
5. Vary the activity:
   - Walk on tiptoes
   - Walk on heels
   - Walk, stop, and balance on one foot briefly, then continue; repeat.
   - Ask the children for their ideas of how to walk the line.

Expand It!

After each child tries the activity, put the children in groups and set up several similar lines going at once.

Rock the Boat

Stretch and tone core stomach muscles and back muscles.

How to Do It

1. Ask the children to lie flat on the floor on their tummies. Tell them they will rock back and forth, pretending to be boats in the water.
2. Ask them to reach their hands around and behind their bodies and grab their ankles or feet.
3. Encourage them to rock forward and back.
4. Encourage them to rock side to side.
5. Encourage them to rock all around in a circle.
6. Encourage them to make big boat-horn sounds: *Honk! Honk!*

Airplane

This exercise for spinal extension builds the muscles along the back and neck while stretching the muscles along the front of the body.

How to Do It

1. Tell the children that they will pretend to be airplanes. Ask the children to lie on their bellies with their arms reaching out beside them and their heads down on the floor or mats.
2. Count to three and ask them to lift their faces to focus forward.
3. Ask them to lift their arms a few inches above the floor and pretend they are flying. If they would like, they can make airplane noises as they pretend to soar through the sky.
4. Encourage them to lift their shoulders and upper bodies to stretch the front of the body and engage the back muscles.
5. Ask them to lower their bodies and relax.
6. Repeat, this time extending the feet off of the floor a few inches to use the backs of the legs; then relax.

Expand It!

If the children are interested in superheroes, capitalize on this interest by encouraging them to pretend to fly like their favorite superheroes.

Humpty Dumpty

Improve core strength and directional learning.

How to Do It

1. Ask the children to sit on the floor with enough room around them that they do not hit or run into each other.
2. Teach the children the following rhyme:
   Humpty Dumpty sat on a wall.
   Humpty Dumpty had a great fall.
   All the king's horses
   And all the king's men
   Couldn't put Humpty together again.
3. Next, repeat the rhyme and teach them the following movements:
   Humpty Dumpty sat on a wall. (Sit cross-legged)
   Humpty Dumpty had a great fall. (Rock side to side, pushing off floor with hands)
   All the king's horses (Hug knees, rock forward and back)
   And all the king's men
   Couldn't put Humpty together again. (Rock side to side)

Plane-Train-Truck Game

Develop cardio fitness while improving coordination and kinetic and spatial awareness.

How to Do It

1. Ask the children to line up on one side of the room. Tell them that you will call out the name of a vehicle and they will pretend to be that vehicle as they move across the room.
2. Call out a vehicle, such as an airplane. Encourage the children to make airplane arms straight out to the sides and to swoop around, changing levels as they "fly" across the room.
3. Call out several vehicles and encourage the children to make noises and movements that they think match that vehicle:
   - Train—Make "choo-choo" arms and march across floor
   - Dump truck—Get down on all fours and crawl across the floor, lifting the upper body as if dumping out dirt
   - Plow—Start with arms at sides in a low V shape, fingers open and out; slowly trudge across the floor as they pretend to sift through dirt
   - Crane—Face forward with hands and feet on the floor and bottoms lifted in a "crab walk" position, with feet leading first; as they move across floor, children lift up one leg and then the other for the boom or arm of crane
   - Jackhammer—Stand and bounce knees quickly, then hop across floor, using hands to hold onto the handle
   - Bulldozer—Start seated with legs out and knees slightly bent, scootch along on bottoms, and pretend to scoop up the dirt with arms

Ball Bounce Cardio

Using an imaginary ball gives cardio benefits and ball-handling skills without a ball to drop and pick up.

How to Do It

1. Ask the children to line up on one side of the room. Tell them that they will pretend to carry imaginary balls as they move across the room.
2. Ask the children to pick up their imaginary balls.
3. Ask them to run across the room while pretending to bounce a ball. Encourage them as they move.
4. Next, ask them to pretend to bounce a ball across the room and then shoot a basket.
5. Ask them to side-gallop while pretending to bounce a ball.
6. Ask them to gallop or run while pretending to throw a ball in the air and then catch it.
7. Ask them to gallop or run while pretending to toss the ball from hand to hand.

Expand It!

When the children are comfortable with pretending to bounce a ball as they move, add music and encourage them to move to the beat.

Boing, Boing, Pop!

Use children's love of bubbles in this cardiovascular exercise.

How to Do It

1. Ask the children to sit in a circle. Encourage them to hold their hands up to their mouths and pretend to blow a big bubble in the middle of the circle. Count how many breaths it takes to blow up the imaginary bubble. Encourage the children to tell you how big they think the bubble is.
2. Ask them to bend their knees and to hold their hands up, pretending to push against the side of the bubble with their hands and feet. Say, "Boing!" as you push, and pretend the bubble has knocked you backward. Encourage the children to roll onto their backs and back up into a seated position.
3. After three tries, encourage them to pretend the bubble has popped and to roll onto their backs. Say, "Pop!" and roll back.
4. Try the activity standing. Bounce up and down as you move around in a circle with the children. Say, "Boing, boing, boing," as you bounce around.
5. Say, "Pop!" as you clap your hands loudly. Encourage the children to pretend to pop. Ask them to show you what they think a popped bubble looks like.
6. Continue in this manner as long as the children are interested.

Let's Get Active!

Research suggests that children who have high levels of physical activity have better motor skills than children who do not engage in high levels of physical activity.

Make an X; Make an I

Encourage cardiovascular exercise while children develop gross motor skills.

How to Do It

1. Show the children what the letter *X* looks like (use a picture or draw one for them). Show them what the letter *I* looks like. Tell the children they will make an *X* and then an *I* with their bodies.
2. Make a big *X* with your body by jumping with your feet out and arms extended. Encourage the children to do the same.
3. Make an *I* by jumping to bring your feet together, and stand tall with hands at your side. Encourage the children to do the same.
4. Bend forward and touch your toes. Come back up to standing.
5. Repeat several times with the children: "Make an *X*! Make an *I*! Now, bend!"

Expand It!

Play some music and encourage the children to do the exercise to the beat.

Over, Under, Around, and Through

Create an obstacle course to reinforce gross motor skills, eye-hand coordination, and spatial awareness.

How to Do It

1. Create an obstacle course using small and medium mats, flat rubber dots, wedges, tape lines, hula hoops, cones or buckets, and tunnels. If you do not have these props in your classroom, be creative with what you do have: crawl under tables, weave around chairs, make a tunnel out of a large appliance box, and so on. Children should have to weave their bodies over, under, around, and through the course.

2. Create a clear start point and end point. Set up a variety of obstacles:
   - Small mats—leap over, hop onto, twirl or spin on, freestyle movement, or dance on
   - Medium mats—roll, crawl, march, tip-toe, or walk with giant steps along
   - Flat rubber dots—hop along, use as stepping stones
   - Hula hoops—jump into, hula with, wiggle in
   - Tape line—walk and balance along, walk sideways on (step together), hop along on one foot
   - Wedge—walk up and leap off, crawl up, roll down, balance on
   - Cones—weave around, walk between, crawl or slither between

3. You may also choose to use existing features of your classroom as stations:
   - Scarves—grab and move to a bucket, hold and twirl, leap with
   - Area rug—hop onto, leap over, freestyle movement and dance
   - Alphabet wall—touch toes, jump with feet open and closed, wiggle, gallop past
   - Front door—take a bow, low kicks, pump arms, march in a circle
   - Windows—wiggle, walk sideways
   - Child's own seat or table—hop on one foot in front of
   - Tiled floor—tap dance, fast feet
   - Carpeted floor—slow motion run, leap, crawl or slither on belly, log-roll

4. Demonstrate how to follow the course, then ask the children to move through the course one at a time. Help them as they go, if they need direction or encouragement.

Expand It!

Once the children understand this exercise, allow them to help design the order of the course and the tasks to perform at each landmark.

Jump Rope Exercise

Improve cardiovascular fitness and coordination by pretending to jump rope. This prepares the muscle memory for the children to actually jump rope when they are older.

How to Do It

1. Do this exercise with a steady, even beat. You can clap or play music to establish a rhythm.
2. Ask the children to stand with space around them so they can move safely.
3. Begin clapping and ask the children to clap with you, or start the music.
4. Hold your elbows at your sides as if you are holding a jump rope.
5. Jump up and down, pretending to swing the rope around by making a circle using your wrists. Count to eight two times.
6. When the children are comfortable with the movement, try jumping forward and back, counting to eight two times.
7. Try jumping side to side, counting to eight two times.

Expand It!

Try speeding up the tempo. See how fast the children can jump.

Hip Hop Dance

Encourage coordination, gross motor development, and listening skills.

How to Do It

1. Ask the children to spread out around the room and to face you.
2. Turn with your back to the children to demonstrate the steps.
3. Choose one step at a time, and demonstrate for the children:
   - Hands on hips, jump feet widely apart, then bring feet together
   - Jump up and reach fingers to the sky, then land in a crouched position on the floor (like a ball)
   - Spin to the right
   - Spin to the left
4. Encourage the children to do the steps with you.
5. When the children are comfortable with the steps, encourage them to add steps of their own.

Expand It!

Divide the class into groups of three. Ask them to make a formation like a triangle, and encourage each trio to perform the dance for fellow classmates.

Ready, Set, Go!

Encourage cardiovascular health and endurance through this fun game.

How to Do It

1. Ask the children to line up on one side of the room. Tell them that they will run to the other side of the room and do a task, then run back as fast as they can.
2. Start with a simple task, such as running across the room and then touching a toe to the wall at the other side. Encourage the children to do the activity one at a time.
3. Vary the activity by changing the task:
   - Run and put two hands and two feet on the floor at the other end of the room
   - Run and put two hands and one foot on the floor with the other leg in the air
   - Run and put two hands on the floor, kicking the feet up in the air
4. Vary the activity by changing how the children move across the room:
   - turn in circles
   - gallop
   - jump
   - hop

Expand It!

Place different-colored scarves at the opposite wall, and call out one color at a time. Encourage the children to run and grab that specific color of scarf and twirl it as they come back.

In "Moving with the Brain in Mind," Eric Jensen says that movement increases the heart rate and circulation, enhances spatial learning, and stimulates the release of beneficial chemicals, as it affirms the value of implicit learning—learning that involves children's creative decisions and actions.

Touch Your Toes; Touch Your Nose

Help the children increase flexibility and motor control.

How to Do It

1. Ask the children to sit on the floor in a circle.
2. Encourage the children to stretch their legs out in front of them. Ask them to lean over and touch their toes with both hands.
3. Ask the children to sit up and touch their noses with both hands.
4. Move your hands from your nose out in a wide circle away from your body, all the way around until you hide your hands behind your back. Encourage the children to copy you.
5. Ask them, "Where are your fingers hiding? Nobody knows! Let's count to three and you can surprise me! Count with me: One, two, three!" You and the children quickly bring your hands to the front and say, "Surprise!"
6. Repeat this sequence several times, as long as the children are interested.

Expand It!

Increase and decrease the speed of the parts of the exercise to increase the surprise and humor.

Row, Row, Row Your Boat

Reinforce cross-body patterning with this familiar song.

How to Do It

1. Ask the children to stand in the center of the room. Tell them that you will pretend to go on a boat ride. Pretend to put on life vests, clicking the clasps and tightening the straps. Ask the children to sit down in your pretend boat and pick up a paddle.
2. Teach the children the following song, pretending to paddle along as you sing:
   Row, row, row your boat
   Gently down the stream
   Merrily, merrily, merrily, merrily
   Life is but a dream.
3. Repeat the song, pretending to paddle on one side, and then the other.
4. As the children continue to paddle, ask them where they think the boat is going. Let them tell you where you will go, what you will see along the way, and what you will do when you arrive.

Skip to My Lou

Galloping or running and galloping typically precede skipping. When children are ready to transfer weight from one foot to another in a skipping pattern, they will be able to successfully do the movement. For now, any rhythmic response to the directions is appropriate.

How to Do It

1. Ask the children to sit in a circle. Teach them the following song:
   (Chorus)
   Lou, Lou, skip to my Lou.
   Lou, Lou, skip to my Lou.
   Lou, Lou, skip to my Lou.
   Skip to my Lou, my darlin'.

   Fly's in the buttermilk,
   Shoo, fly, shoo!
   Fly's in the buttermilk,
   Shoo, fly, shoo!
   Fly's in the buttermilk,
   shoo, fly, shoo!
   Skip to my Lou, my darlin'.
   (Chorus)

2. Ask the children to stand in a circle with their hands on their hips. Show them how to step and hop, step and hop. Ask them to try the movement.

3. Ask them to step, and hop in one direction around the circle. Start by singing slowly so children hear your words as they move. When you say, "Skip to my Lou," the children can run, walk, or gallop.
   Step hop, step hop, skip to my Lou,
   Step hop, step hop, skip to my Lou,
   Step hop, step hop, skip to my Lou,
   Skip to my Lou, my darlin'.

4. When the children are comfortable with the movement, try picking up the tempo a bit.

Growing Trees

Help the children develop core strength and learn to stretch from the ground to a standing position.

How to Do It

1. Ask the children to lie on their backs in the center of the room. Tell them they will each pretend to be a tree that grows up from the ground.
2. Tell them that, at first, they are little seedlings, growing up out of the ground from a seed. Ask them to pretend to slowly unwind and wiggle out of the ground toward the sun. Give them time to explore this movement.
3. Tell them that now they are growing bigger. They are little trees, reaching toward the sky. Encourage them to spread out their branches and leaves in the sun as they slowly grow.
4. Tell them they are big trees now. Encourage them to stretch very high and to stand tall. When the wind blows, they gently sway side to side. Give them time to explore these movements.

Twisting

Stretch the muscles of the spine and hips, and encourage cross-body patterning.

How to Do It

1. Ask the children to stand in the center of the room. They may put their hands on their hips, or they may choose to hold their arms out at their sides.
2. Show them how to twist from the waist. Let them explore that movement with you.
3. Add a knee bend as you twist. Encourage them to bend their knees and twist as low as they can.
4. Encourage them to twist back up to standing.
5. Continue in this manner, adding some music for them to twist to.

Wiggle, Wiggle

Encourage the children to name their body parts and explore how their body parts move.

How to Do It

1. Ask the children to sit in a circle. Tell them that you will call out specific body parts, and encourage them to move that body part when they hear its name.

2. Call out body parts, and let the children explore different ways to move those parts:
   - Fingers: wiggle, shake, point
   - Arm: shake, wave, flap
   - Foot: wiggle, roll in a circle, step, stomp, point
   - Leg: lift, kick, shake
   - Tummy: wiggle, stick out and in
   - Head: nod, shake, turn
   - Knee: wiggle, shake, bend
   - Whole body: encourage the children to wiggle their entire bodies

Expand It!

Go around in a circle and repeat the list. Encourage each child to show the class how they choose to move one body part differently from the other children.

Little Robots

Encourage the children to explore body control through stiff robot actions.

How to Do It

1. Ask the children to stand well spaced in the room. Ask them if they have ideas about how a robot might talk and move. Tell them that robots move stiffly, because they are usually made of metal and hard plastic. Give two or three children a chance to tell or show you how a robot might move or talk.
2. Encourage the children to move stiffly, perhaps walking with straight legs and holding their arms in a rigid position.
3. Encourage the children to bend stiffly from their hips or knees, to turn or sit.
4. Encourage them to dance like robots.

Expand It!

Divide the class into partners or trios and encourage them to create a robot dance together.

This Little Light of Mine

Use a verse of this familiar song to encourage understanding of directional movement and coordination.

How to Do It

1. Ask the children to sit in a circle. Teach them the following verse from "This Little Light of Mine," written by Harry Dixon Loes (ca. 1920):
   This little light of mine,
   I'm gonna let it shine.
   This little light of mine,
   I'm gonna let it shine.
   This little light of mine,
   I'm gonna let it shine.
   Let it shine.
   Let it shine.
   Let it shine.

2. Ask the children to form a line in the center of the room. Explain that they will use their pointer fingers to pretend to point a light in the direction they move.

3. Encourage them to sing the song, pointing as they move:
   This little light of mine, (Point forward, take three steps forward)
   I'm gonna let it shine. (Point back over shoulder, take three steps back)
   This little light of mine, (Point right, take three steps right)
   I'm gonna let it shine. (Point left, take three steps left)
   This little light of mine, (Point forward, take three steps forward)
   I'm gonna let it shine. (Point back over shoulder, take three steps back)
   Let it shine. (Point right, walk around in a circle clockwise)
   Let it shine. (Point left, walk in a circle counterclockwise)
   Let it shine. (Point right, walk in a circle clockwise)

Use directional words such as *right, left, forward, backward, over, under, below, near, on, in, around, outside, inside, behind,* and so on with the children as you move. Through connecting the movement with the word, they will learn the meanings of these words and add them to their vocabularies.

Look for Kitten!

Help children develop spatial awareness and directional vocabulary through a variation of Hide and Seek.

How to Do It

1. Before the exercise begins, hide a stuffed animal or other toy somewhere in your classroom where the children will be able to search for it.
2. Ask the children to sit with you on the rug. Tell them that you have noticed that one of the stuffed animals, Kitten*, is missing. (*Substitute the name of the toy you choose.) Tell them, "I know Kitten is in this classroom somewhere! Where could she be?"
3. Ask the children to offer suggestions for where the toy might be. If they are not sure where to start, offer some ideas and encourage the children to look in each spot as you name it: Is she under the table? behind the door? below the sink? near the chalkboard? on the bookshelf? in the wastebasket? under the desk? outside the window? inside the cabinet?
4. Make sure that the last place you name is the hiding spot. When the children find the toy, ask them to bring it back to the circle.

Expand It!

Let each child take a turn hiding Kitten for the class to find.

Let's Breathe In and Out

Help the children learn a simple way to calm themselves.

How to Do It

1. Ask the children to sit or stand. Sitting is more relaxing; standing helps the children refocus to move on quickly to another activity.
2. Ask the children to raise their arms in the air and reach for the sky.
3. Ask them to take a deep breath in but not to hold their breath. Ask them to breathe out and drop their arms.
4. Repeat two more times.

Expand It!

Invite the children to lie down on the floor and do the exercise as a brief rest period or as the beginning of nap time.

Breathe In, Breathe Out—I'm Calm

Provide a tool for the children to relax themselves, as a group or individually.

How to Do It

1. This activity can be done anytime: sitting at tables, standing in line, or sitting in a group.
2. Ask the children to reach up as they take a breath in and to lower their arms as they breathe out, repeating two times.
3. On the third breath, ask them to raise their arms again, but cross their arms to give themselves a hug as they breathe out.

Teach breathing as a tool that can be used by any child when he or she feels the need to calm down.

Calming Head and Hands

Encourage concentration and focus through this calming exercise.

How to Do It

1. Ask the children to sit with you. Model the movements for them, and encourage them to copy you.
2. Ask them to put their hands on their heads and give their heads a nice little rub.
3. Keep one hand on your head and put your other hand on your heart. Tell the children, "Your lungs are here in your chest. Breathe in (pause) and out."
4. Keep that hand on your head and put your other hand on your tummy. Breathe in (pause) and out.
5. Keep that hand on your head and find your belly button. Breathe in (pause) and out.
6. Put both hands back on your head and give your head a nice little rub.
7. Change hands, putting the other hand on your heart. Repeat the exercises with the children.

Laughing

Laughing is a great way to relax and release tension.

How to Do It

1. Start by making laughing sounds. Giggle or chuckle—you will be surprised at how quickly the children begin to join in. Laughter is contagious!
2. Let the whole group just get those giggles out for a few minutes.
3. Lead the children in taking a few deep breaths to calm down and refocus.

Squeeze, Please, and Say, "Ha!"

Help the children relax and calm themselves after physical activity.

How to Do It

1. Ask the children to lie on their backs. Tell them they will take a little rest, but first they will use their muscles.
2. Ask them to close their eyes.
3. Tell them to squeeze the part of the body you call out and then relax it and say, "Ha!"
   - Squeeze your eyes and mouth—squeeze them tightly. Now open them softly and say, "Ha!"
   - Squeeze your arms and hands. Make fists with your hands and use your muscles. Now let them go and say, "Ha!"
   - Squeeze your legs and feet. Squeeze up your toes and use your muscles. Now let them go and say, "Ha!"
   - Squeeze everything on your body. Squeeze and use your muscles. Now let everything go and say, "Ha!"

Let's Put Away Our Action Parts

Help the children wind down after physical activity.

How to Do It

1. Ask the children to sit in a circle. Tell them that it is time to put away their action bodies for now.
2. Tell them to find their pretend pockets so they can put the parts in.
3. First, tell them to put away their listening ears. Encourage them to touch their ears and pretend to put them away. Say, "Ding, ding, ding, ding, ding."
4. Tell them, "Let's put away our watching eyes." Encourage them to touch their eyelids and pretend to put them away.
5. Say, "Let's put away our funny nose—Boop!" Encourage them to touch their noses and pretend to put them away.
6. Encourage them to touch their mouths, making a "wawawa" sound by tapping their mouths. Put their mouths away.
7. Tell them, "Let's put away our big feet!" They should bend their knees and tap their toes on the floor.
8. Tell them to put away their tiny feet by tapping on the floor with tiny, quiet beats of their toes.
9. Tell them to put away their flying arms and fingers by making their arms fly and their fingers flutter in fluid motions.
10. Say, "Everything is put away in our pretend pockets! I am ready to rest now, and I see you are, too." Take a deep breath in and out, and say, "Ha!"

Expand It!

Add other body parts to put away, such as the tummy, balancing feet, or elbows.

Resources

Alvers, Emily. 2011. "Safety Tips for Stretching Exercises for Kids." Livestrong.com.
http://www.livestrong.com/article/105177-safety-tips-stretching-exercises-kids/.

Bransford, John, Ann Brown, and Rodney Cocking, eds. 2000. *How People Learn: Brain, Mind, Experience, and School.* 2nd ed. Washington, DC: National Academy Press.

Brownell, Kelly, and Katherine Horgen. 2004. *Food Fight: The Inside Story of the Food Industry, America's Obesity Crisis, and What We Can Do about It.* New York: McGraw-Hill.

Carlson, Frances M. 2011. *Big Body Play.* Washington, DC: National Association for the Education of Young Children.

Cohen, Bonnie B. 2008. *Sensing, Feeling, and Action,* 2nd ed. Northampton, MA: Contact Editions.

Deiner, Penny L., and Wei Qui. 2007. "Embedding Physical Activity and Nutrition in Early Care and Educational Programs." *Zero to Three* (28)1: 13–18.

Department of Health and Human Services. *President's Council on Fitness, Sports, and Nutrition.* http://www.fitness.gov.

Elliot, Eloise, and Steve Sanders. 2002. "Children and Physical Activity: The Importance of Movement and Physical Activity." PBS Teachers.
http://www.pbs.org/teachers/earlychildhood/articles/physical.html

Fast Food F.A.C.T.S. Food Advertising to Children and Teens Score.
http://fastfoodmarketing.org/.

Gearhardt, Ashley, Sonja Yokum, Patrick Orr, Eric Stice, William Corbin, and Kelly Gerber, F. Joyce. 2008. *Teaching with Heart.* Bridgeport, CT: Teaching with Heart LLC Publications.

Hannaford, Carla. 2005. *Smart Moves: Why Learning Is Not All in Your Head,* 2nd ed. Arlington, VA: Great Ocean.

Harris, Jennifer, Marlene Schwartz, Amy Ustjanauskas, Punam Ohri-Vachaspati, and Kelly Brownell. 2011. "Effects of Serving High-sugar Cereals on Children's Breakfast-eating Behavior." *Pediatrics* 127(1): 71–76.

Jensen, Eric. 2000. "Moving with the Brain in Mind." *Educational Leadership* 58(3): 34–37.

Kenney, Erica, Kathryn Henderson, Debbie Humphries, Marlene Schwartz. 2011. "Practice-based Research to Engage Teachers and Improve Nutrition in the Preschool Setting." *Childhood Obesity* 7(6): 475–479.

Larson, Nicole, Dianne Ward, Sara Neelon, and Mary Story. 2011. *Preventing Obesity among Preschool Children: How Can Child-care Settings Promote Healthy Eating and Physical Activity?* Princeton, NJ: Robert Wood Johnson Foundation.

National Association for Sports and Physical Education. 2009. *Active Start: A Statement of Physical Activity Guidelines for Children from Birth to Age 5*. 2nd ed. Reston, VA: NASPE.

O'Connell, Megan, Kathryn Henderson, Joerg Luedicke, and Marlene Schwartz. 2012. "Repeated Exposure in a Natural Setting: A Preschool Intervention to Increase Vegetable Consumption." *Journal of the Academy of Nutrition and Dietetics* (112)2: 230–234.

Olds, Anita. 1994. "From Cartwheels to Caterpillars: Children's Need to Move Indoors and Out." *Building Opportunities for Gross Motor Development* (97): 32–36.

Pica, Rae. 2007. *Jump into Literacy: Active Learning for Preschool Children*. Beltsville, MD: Gryphon House.

Pica, Rae. 2008. *Jump into Math: Active Learning for Preschool Children*. Beltsville, MD: Gryphon House.

Pica, Rae. 2009. *Jump into Science: Active Learning for Preschool Children*. Beltsville, MD: Gryphon House.

Pica, Rae. 2006. *Moving and Learning Across the Curriculum*, 2nd edition. Independence, KY: Wadsworth.

President's Council on Physical Fitness and Sports. 2000. "Current Issues in Flexibility Fitness." *Research Digest* 3(10): 5.

Puhl, Rebecca. 2011. "Weight Stigmatization toward Youth: A Significant Problem in Need of Societal Solutions." *Childhood Obesity* 7(5): 359–363.

Ratey, John. 2008. *Spark: The Revolutionary New Science of Exercise and the Brain*. New York: Little, Brown.

Singer, Dorothy, and Jerome Singer. 2005. *Imagination and Play in the Electronic Age*. Cambridge, MA: Harvard University Press.

Tanofsky-Kraff, Marian, Ann F. Haynos, Lisa A. Kotler, Susan Z. Yanovski, and Jack A. Yanovski. 2007. "Laboratory-Based Studies of Eating among Children and Adolescents." *Current Nutrition and Food Science* (3)1: 55–74.

Timmons, Brian, Patti-Jean Naylor, and Karin Pfeiffer. 2007. "Physical Activity for Preschool Children—How Much and How?" *Applied Physiology, Nutrition, and Metabolism* 32(S2E): S122–S134.

U.S. Department of Agriculture. Choose My Plate. http://www.choosemyplate.gov/

Wardle, Francis. n.d. "Play as Curriculum." *Early Childhood News*. http://www.earlychildhoodnews.com/earlychildhood/article_view.aspx?ArticleID=127.

Willis, Judy. 2008. *How Your Child Learns Best: Brain-Friendly Strategies You Can Use to Ignite Your Child's Learning and Increase School Success*. Naperville, IL: Sourcebooks.

Yale Rudd Center for Food Policy and Obesity. Yale University. www.yaleruddcenter.org/.

Index